50 Years of Fleet Street

50 Years of Fleet Street

L. W. 'BILL' NEEDHAM

LONDON
MICHAEL JOSEPH

First published in Great Britain by Michael Joseph Ltd
52 Bedford Square, London, W.C.1
1973

ISBN 0 7181 1088 9

Set and printed in Great Britain by
Tonbridge Printers Ltd, Peach Hall Works, Tonbridge, Kent
in Plantin eleven on thirteen point on paper supplied by
P. F. Bingham Ltd, and bound by James Burn
at Esher, Surrey

Contents

Illustrations

CHAPTER ONE

Down the Inky Way

'The Street of Adventure' Beckons – Boyhood in a Rural Suburb of London – The Cricklewood Horse-Bus – 'The Major' And Our First Motor Omnibus – My Dive into The Street Of Ink

On a dark night of stars, at one in the morning a thunderous knock on the front door shook the small house. A dog barked. Far off in a field a cow mooed mournfully. Outside, on the dusty, rutted road a horse pawed restlessly. Little bells jangled. Again the thunderous knock reverberated through the dark house.

My mother and father stirred in their bed, one of those big, Victorian brass double-beds with rails and knobs at either end. They sat up and whispered. I, in my small bed, quivered with apprehension and curiosity. This was a drama of a dark, sinister sort on a dark and undoubtedly sinister night. A burglar? A highwayman? Nothing less could happen in the dark fantasy of that sudden alarm in a sleeping village under the stars.

My father got out of bed, threw on a dressing gown and marched downstairs. In my mind's eye I saw him clutching a cudgel or a pistol – which, so far as I remember, he did not possess – ready to meet the midnight raider. He flung open the door.

Outside, in the half-light of winking stars and a guttering oil lamp perched on its iron stalk, a London hansom-cab stood at the garden gate. The driver touched his bowler hat to my father and said, 'There's a gentleman to see you, sir. He's come in my cab all the way from Fleet Street in London.'

The gentleman from Fleet Street, in a few brief urgent phrases, begged my father to get into the cab at once and go with him at top speed, which meant one-horse speed, to the dark mystery of London. Its lights winked in the far distance, below the high ground on which sprawled our country village of Cricklewood. My father dressed hurriedly, kissed my mother goodbye and murmured; 'This is dreadful. I must go at once. I can't think what they've been up to.'

My mother burst into tears. I, goggle-eyed in my woolly

9

dressing-gown, sobbed in unison. I was convinced that my dear papa was about to be whisked off to the Tower of London and there led to the block to face the headsman's axe, or, if not that dramatic fate, that he would land up in jail, anyway. He was back in time for breakfast.

Now this dramatic episode on a dark night in the last year of Queen Victoria's reign, changed my whole life. It set me on a career in Fleet Street which dates from that day.

Let us go back to the beginning. Cricklewood at the turn of the century was a placid country village set among hedges, bright in June with dogroses, and grass fields dappled with buttercups and cows. The roads were dusty. The fields paths were muddy. Suburbia was just beginning to creep out from London. A few new brick houses, of which ours was one, nudged the old country cottages of mellow red-brick or white-painted clapboard, with roofs of wavy, red shingles or sun-warmed tiles. Cricklewood was still a village of peace and rural philosophy.

The Crown Inn, ancient, sprawling, with dormer windows, tipsy eaves and roof-trees was compounded of the quirks and architectural fantasies of several centuries. It was the club to which all right-thinking and 'long-headed' farmers and farm labourers, cowmen, ploughmen, hedgers and ditchers belonged. Like every other country pub, no woman was ever seen in it, and no small boys were admitted. Today that old pub of peace has been swept away. A large, red-brick Edwardian hostelry with bars and restaurants, bright lights and bright young people has taken its place.

At the village cross-road, a wooden sign-post with four white-painted arms directed one to London, Hampstead, Willesden and Hendon. A traffic circus, a vortex of unending vehicles, noise and din has taken its place. Motor-buses and trams have ousted the carrier's cart. The butcher's high-wheeled semi-dog cart with its fast trotter which he drove in a blue and white striped apron with a yellowy-white straw hat rammed down over his ears, with all the panache of a Bertram Mills, is a museum-piece. The broughams and landaus of the local gentry, most of them rich city merchants, have gone with the wind. Their coachmen with cockades in their shining top-hats are a memory for men of seventy years or more, as are the little boys, the 'tigers' who sat dutifully beside them, arms folded, in neat livery. Cricklewood today is just another suburb.

Where the cows grazed in those boyhood days and we went birds-nesting along hedgerows bright with dog-roses, there are engineering works, great motor works, factory chimneys and the hum and bustle of industry.

I wonder what 'the major' would say to it all if he were to return for a brief apoplectic moment. He was my boyhood hero. He drove the horse-bus with its pair of spanking carriage horses which left the Crown early each morning to the barking of dogs and general excitement, on its six-mile or so journey to Marble Arch. It did that trip several times each day. It was the commuter-service of seventy years ago.

'The major' had been, not, I think a major but more probably a troop sergeant-major in that crack cavalry corps, the Blues. He had retired with an active mind, a hardy body and an enduring love of the horse. Thus he became the driver of the Cricklewood to London horse-bus. No road coachman of the eighteenth century, driving his spanking team down to Brighton in the days when Prinny was in his heyday, no Sir Vincent Cotton or Squire Osbaldston could have cut a bigger figure in popular estimation than 'the major' cut in my five-year-old appraisal. There was a hero.

I see him now, erect, soldierly, red-faced, clad in a three-tiered greatcoat of the sort that Sam Weller might have worn, a brown Derby hat rammed down over his ears, his long driving whip with its neatly furled lash, striding off to mount the high seat in the front of the bus whilst an ostler held the two horses by the head. Favoured passengers were allowed on the driving seat to sit beside 'the major'. That was the ultimate honour.

Alas, the poor old 'major's' brief reign of equine glory was cut short when the first motor-bus, a green-and-white single-decker monster, 'The Pioneer', was put on the road. It banged, snorted, hissed, rattled and smoked. It terrified 'the major's' two spanking horses out of their wits. They reared up on either side of the pole. They kicked over the traces. They went down on their knees and barked them badly. They even bolted with 'the major' hanging on to the reins, cursing with parade-ground ferocity. In the end it was too much. He gave up.

Now on that dark night which, as I say, decided my career, my father, who was the manager of a firm which made box-wood blocks for newspaper illustrations, had been called out of his bed because his principal customer, the *Illustrated London News* had lost the blocks for the edition just about to go to press. A catastrophe of the first magnitude whose awful significance only a newspaper-man could truly appreciate. It is equivalent to losing the bridegroom when the bride is already at the altar. Some blockhead in the printing works had justified his blockishness by losing the blocks. So at one o'clock in the morning, father had to leave his warm bed and go off to the dark mysteries of Fleet Street to find the blocks and start the presses thundering. I heard all about it at breakfast-time.

The urgency, the drama, the romance and, in a sense, the mystery of Fleet Street, 'The Street of Adventure' seized my mind. It was made up as I delved into the breakfast egg. Fleet Street was the street for me. The Street of Adventure. The street where every second was charged with drama. Never a dull moment. After more than fifty years of it 'The Street', to me, is still the hub of adventure.

Adventure decided my school for me. My father with a charity and understanding perhaps rare among the parents of the day gave me the choice of going either to the Haberdashers School which was not far from home, or to a large school of some six hundred boys in the City of London. I plumped for the latter. For the reason that it meant the daily joyous adventure of travelling from Cricklewood to Moorgate Street on a 'puffing billy' train, a clanking crocodile of coaches drawn by a coal-fired steam-locomotive which belched clouds of black smoke, hissed jets of white steam and occasionally let out a blood-curdling whistle. To travel behind that apparition was a morning joy and an afternoon ecstasy.

One's schooldays may be either a precious memory or an insufferable nightmare. In any case they tend to bore the average reader. So I will merely say that if we erred, as any right-minded boy will do, we were caned. We had no neurotic frenzies about it as so many bogus-intellectual writers are inclined to remember today. If we got the cane we knew we deserved it. So we gritted our teeth and put up with it. The main thing that kept me personally on the path of comparative rectitude was the knowledge that if anyone was going to raise weals on my backside it would be either the Headmaster or, of all people, 'the major'. This was not my horse-driving hero, but another old soldier whose job was to maintain discipline on the playing fields at Stamford Hill and in the school playground. He stopped bullying among the boys. He settled the inevitable squabbles with rough, swift justice. He drilled a sense of discipline into us all. I was frightened of him, but respected him. One recognised that his justice, though rough, was just.

Came the day when 'the major', unwittingly, was the fairy godfather of us all. His daughter ran the school tuck-shop. There she dispensed boiled sweets wrapped up in frilly papers. You got a dozen for a penny, half a dozen for a halfpenny or three for a farthing. Farthings and halfpennys were potent coinage in schoolboy economy. I still remember the delicious moment when my half dozen or dozen were carefully counted out and I slipped the copper coin across the counter.

Then the daughter fell ill. 'The major', anxious that the family should not lose the tuck-shop profits, took over the shop. He could not be bothered to count out the sweets. Instead you offered your penny and he gave you a handful. As his hands were half as large as umbrellas one got a rare bonus. The word flew round the school. By the end of the day the tuck-shop had lost its entire stock of sweets – and its profit.

My school major did not, however, impress me so vividly as the horse-bus major. The latter had three pretty daughters. I fell in love with each of them in rapid succession with all the ardour of a five-year-old. Even more, I fell in love with the splendour of his Service helmet. This, a mighty affair of burnished brass, with a magnificent plume of horse-hair, was mounted on a wooden stand on the sideboard in the little dining-room of his house. I gazed at it with awe. It epitomised the might and chivalry of the British Army. One could imagine 'the major' glaring fiercely from beneath that brass helmet, his jaw jutting over the chin-strap, sabre upswung, charging on one of his bus-horses, slap into the middle of Napoleon's Old Guard at Waterloo. The playground major could never come up to that. He had merely been in the Rifle Brigade, quick step, but no galloping horses.

When I was a little older, my father who, as I have said, was manager of a block-making firm, Badereau and Jones of Poppins Court, Fleet Street, had the foresight to see that the wood block was on the way out. The future lay with the zinc stereos such as are used today. He also envisaged the development of electros and stereos. I need not go into further technical detail other than to say that he saw well ahead of his time.

When I was about fifteen he sent me to the School of Lithography and Photo-Engraving in Bolt Court, a narrow alleyway off Fleet Street. We students did a full day of hard work from nine to six. We learnt the practical stuff, including photography in the morning. The early afternoon was taken up by a refresher course in normal scholastic work. This was followed by an hour or so of sketching and line drawing using live models. I have always had a liking for painting and drawing and I like to remember that I made so much progress that I became the youngest student to be allowed to take part in the life classes in the evening. Drawing has been one of my hobbies ever since.

I fortunately made so much progress in fine etching which appealed to me enormously that after a while my father was able to find me a job with George Newnes, Ltd., as an improver in the fine-etching department of the block-making division which served their chain of magazines. These included *Country Life*, *The Strand Magazine*, and one or two other high-class magazines with *Tit-Bits* as a popular money-earner. To this day I remember with a certain pride that more than once I 'painted in' clouds on a blue sky for colour blocks which later embellished *Country Life*.

Then came the outbreak of the First World War on August 4th, 1914. I was nineteen years of age. The world was my oyster so far as block-making was concerned, but a far wider world opened to my vision when the first rifle-shots were fired.

CHAPTER TWO

First World War

The Deadly Sting in Britain's Tail – I Join The Artists' Rifles and
Miss Death by a Fluke – Trench Warfare at its Worst – German
Buried Alive – Nearly Half of Us Wiped Out – I Get the M.C. –
'On a Dark Night All Hell Broke Loose' – I Defy the General – 'Ypres
Where Peace Never Reigned' – The Greatest Blow-Up of All Time –
Hill 60 – Man-Eating Rats – I Meet My Waterloo

The outbreak of war on August 4th, 1914 hit Britain like a
thunderclap. There had been no great European war, involving
this country, for a century. Napoleon was the last mighty enemy.
Now the England of top-hats and frock-coats, carriages and
hansom-cabs, straw boaters and pushbikes, of dukes and dustmen,
had to face the most highly disciplined army in Europe. The
Kaiser's Germany was a faultless military machine. War was its
business, its pride. Each regiment, cavalry, infantry, the guns
and transport were geared to the utmost efficiency. The German
Navy was equally formidable.

The British Army of 100,000 men, small, highly professional
with a tradition of deadly rifle-fire in the Kaiser's words 'A con-
temptible little army.'

The deadly sting in that little army was its incredible fire-
power. Each infantryman was so highly trained in musketry that
he became a living machine-gun. 'Five rounds rapid' was the
mere verbal expression of a rate of fire and accuracy of marks-
manship unparalleled in the world. Every British soldier with a
rifle was, in effect, a crack shot.

Too many of the self-appointed pundits of modern military
history write today denigrating the professional soldiers of the
First World War, particularly the 'officer class'. Most of the
pundits (so-called) were not even born when I and others of my
age went gladly to war. We civilian soldiers, who rushed to join
within days or weeks of that fateful declaration, know well that
we joined a highly efficient fighting machine. It was officered by
men who, in the vast majority, were trained professional soldiers,
with long family tradition behind them. They may have had
'Boer War methods' but that was the only recent war they had

known. They cannot be damned out of hand by the facile critics of today for having failed to realise what a full-scale world war was going to produce in the way of new methods and new strategy. Nobody, here or in Germany, could foresee years of trench warfare. The point which stands out in memory is of the tremendous wave of patriotism which swept the country in those first few weeks of war.

My first reaction was that war had nothing to do with me. It was a job for the professionals. After a few days I changed my mind. Young men everywhere – and middle-aged men – were flocking to the colours. I must be in it. The war would be over by Christmas, in any case. One wonders how many tens of thousands of others thought precisely the same. The supreme self-confidence of the British, something which puzzles and irritates the foreigner, was never better exemplified than in those bright autumn days of 1914. We had declared war against a mighty military power. We were going to win that war. We might have a small army, but it was first-class. We had the finest navy in the world. The British Empire girdled the earth. The sun never set upon it. The all-red route from the Cape to Cairo blazed the path of British sovereignty from one end of Africa to the other. All India was ours. Asia we held in fee. Canada, Australia, New Zealand, South Africa and a hundred small colonies and dependencies were flocking to our aid. The War *must* be over by Christmas.

On September 5th, 1914, with a few shillings in my pocket – I was living on a small allowance from my father during those student days – I hailed a taxi-cab and told the driver to take me to the regimental depot of the 'Westminster' Battalion of the London Division. It was in Buckingham Gate. A queue of men in silk hats and frock-coats, in cloth caps and chokers, in straw boaters and cheap reach-me-downs clustered outside the door. I had to wait my turn. When I finally reached the recruiting sergeant, sitting at a bare wooden table and said I wished to join he asked briefly: 'Name? Age and address?' He wrote down the details. Then he said crisply, 'The First Battalions' full up. We haven't got permission yet to form a Second Battalion. When we have we'll write you.'

I turned on my heel and walked out. I told the taxi-driver to go to the depot of Queen Victoria's Rifles. I got the same reception and the same answer. There followed a dreary progress to the depots of The Honourable Artillery Company who had, and still have, magnificent headquarters in Finsbury with a great grass parade-ground, almost a small park, which today is worth millions in building value. They still stick to their grass. They, too, were full up. So off we went to the London Scottish, and several other Territorial depots. At each place there were the same waiting crowds of would-be soldiers drawn from every class and age group. The same story defeated me at each depot: 'Full up. We'll write later.'

Finally, at the depot of the Artists' Rifles, I was told again that the First Battalion was full and that I would hear in due course. By this time the taxi-cab had clocked up far more money than I had in my pocket. I was desperate. The army could clearly get on without me. The country might be in danger but I was in pawn to the taxi-man. As I came out, despondent, I saw an officer in uniform standing on the pavement watching the would-be volunteers. I knew him. He was a choirister in the church choir at St Gabriel's, Cricklewood where I tuned up my vocal chords as a choir-boy. I went up and said: 'Do you remember me?' He was a man of thirty-odd with two pips and some years' service. It was a toss-up whether he would recognise a fresh-faced choir-boy. If not I was in a mess. Luckily he remembered me. I told him I wanted to join the army quickly but no regiment seemed to want me.

'For Heaven's sake give me a hand,' I pleaded. 'You must have influence. Can you help me get into this regiment?' That touched his sympathy. He scribbled his initials on a slip of paper and said, 'Take that to the medical officer.'

I went back into the building and within a few minutes was before the M.O. He went over me with a stethoscope, and, after a summary examination, said, 'You'll do.'

I went back to my officer-chorister friend and reported, 'The M.O.'s passed me. What do I do now?'

'If he's passed you on my chit, you're a soldier. You'll be called up in a few days. We'll find a corner for you.'

'Thank God,' I ejaculated. Then, overwhelmed with embarrassment, I said, 'I hate to ask you, but I've run up such a taxi bill that I can't afford to pay. Could you possibly lend me a pound?

A pound in those days was equal to more than five pounds today in value. He fished in his pocket and handed me a gold sovereign, a jimmy-o-goblin in the Cockney slang of the day. I paid off the taxi-driver, caught the next 'puffing billy' back to Golders Green to which we had moved and burst in on my family with the glad news. My mother was on the verge of tears. My father was concerned that all the time and money spent on training me to follow in his professional footsteps was now thrown to the wind. Yet he was obviously secretly proud of his son. Those emotions were plain in his face.

Within a few days I was ordered to report to the regimental depot. I turned up with dozens of others, all in our civilian clothes. We were issued with dummy wooden rifles, the sort of things that children would play with. We were marshalled into two ranks and marched off to Russell Square, Bloomsbury for our first taste of training. 'Marched' is a polite euphemism. We had not the faintest idea how to march in step. We were a shambling rabble. For the next few days we were taught to number-off from the right, stick out our chests, throw back our heads, 'look the enemy straight in the eye', form fours and keep in step. The elements of drill.

Before long the shambling civilian rabble took shape as a more or less cohesive group of men and youths who, at the word of command, snapped to attention, squared their shoulders and could march in step. I doubt if one of us had ever fired a rifle before. Few of us knew how to open the breach and slip in a clip of cartridges if we had had breach to open and cartridges to insert. For the time being we were taught how to handle our dummy rifles, to slope arms, ground arms, present arms and to take imaginary aim. We almost began to look like soldiers or, at any rate, military amoebas.

Now, I had an uncle who owned a highly exclusive tailoring business in Savile Row. Normally he tailored dukes and slightly lesser mortals. Uncle George, moved to pity by my unmilitary appearance and perhaps warmed by avuncular pride in the young family soldier, said one day, 'I'll make you a military greatcoat.'

In due course a magnificent khaki greatcoat, gleaming with regimental buttons and red piping arrived at the house in a portentous parcel. I ripped off the string, slipped into the coat – it reached almost to my ankles – and paraded in front of the ecstatic eyes of the family. There was no cap to go with it, no khaki trousers or tunic and certainly no army boots. Nonetheless I could not get to Russell Square quick enough next day to show off my military accoutrement. Proudly garbed, I stood to attention in the front rank, a splendid and arresting figure in my own eyes. Not so to the eyes of my friend, the lieutenant who had lent me the golden sovereign on that fateful day a few weeks earlier. He swivelled an incredulous and baleful eye upon me.

'Where the hell did you get that coat?' he demanded.

'My Uncle George had it made for me, sir,' I replied proudly.

'Then take the damn thing off at once. It's an officer's greatcoat. You're not even a trained private, yet.'

Tears started to my eyes. Shamefacedly I struggled out of the greatcoat. This was disgrace abounding. Then I noticed a twinkle in the lieutenant's eye, a slight quizzical smile. The crime was not so bad after all.

Sadly I took the coat back to Uncle George and explained matters. Off came the regimental buttons and the scarlet piping. The coat was cut down in length and altered to befit my lowly military rank. In the end I was left with a warm, military greatcoat which, although it might not be an official issue was, at any rate, better than anything anyone else had.

A month later we were packed off to two empty mansions at Roehampton not far from the edge of Wimbledon Common. There we were billeted in Roehampton House and Dover House, set in what had been glorious and extensive gardens. They were great country houses on the rural fringe of London. Today Roehampton House is famous as the headquarters of the workshops which provide artificial limbs for crippled soldiers and civilians. Dover House, its lawns and gardens have been obliterated by flats and houses.

We slept in uncarpeted rooms on beds which consisted of

three plain wooden planks with thin straw mattresses and a couple of army blankets which appeared to be made of coconut matting and old wire. This was the hardening-up process.

Most of my companions were professional men: a good sprinkling of doctors, lawyers and accountants with a few writers and actually an artist or two. I believe we could boast a Chelsea sculptor. Most were older than I was and they most definitely had more money to spend. On the whole a decent friendly lot.

Cooking was done on field kitchens. We fed reasonably well on inevitable stews, greasy puddings, prunes and other solid and far from Lucullian fare. Bully beef, later the army stand-by, and its twin sister the tinned Maconochie ration, which almost paved the trenches in France, had not yet loomed on the culinary horizon.

Owing to the high educational standard of the Artists' Rifles there was a constant drain of men who went away to be trained and commissioned as officers. The rest of us, including my youthful self, were in daily demand for fatigue duties. This could mean almost anything from scrubbing the floors or emptying the latrine buckets to scouring the cookhouse pots and pan. I wallowed in grease and filth when one would much rather have been busy with a rifle or learning how to stick a bayonet into a sack-dummy.

Winter was coming on. So with that sublime flair for doing the right thing which distinguishes the army we were hooked out of our bare but windproof and waterproof rooms and put under canvas in tents in Richmond Park. This meant sleeping on ground sheets on the bare ground. The process of hardening-up was accelerated. By this time we had been issued with rifles. They were, if I remember rightly, the old long-barrelled Lee Enfield .303, each of which weighed between nine and ten pounds. We were now in uniform with webbing equipment, trenching tools, billy cans and the rest. Each man's equipment, including rifle, weighed about ninety-six pounds. With this lot on our backs, we dutifully marched five or six miles at a time round the roads and over the bracken-clad slopes of Richmond Park to the eternal wonderment of herds of red and fallow deer which gazed at us wide-eyed in all their antlered beauty.

The tedium of loos and grease was illumined by a machine-gun course. I learned to work – and love – the Maxim machine-gun.

This was pretty well the military marvel of the age. It had been invented a few years before by Sir Hiram Maxim. It was water-cooled and had a rate of fire and accuracy which compared extremely well with the rate of fire of an ordinary infantryman's 'five rounds rapid'. The machine-gun had the advantage of feeding cartridges into the breech not in clips of five but in a continuous belt. It fascinated me. I decided that Needham was to be a machine-gun officer.

I asked my commanding officer for a day's leave to apply for a commission in the Oxford and Bucks Light Infantry. It was granted. Off I went. The C.O. of the Oxford and Bucks informed me that, alas, they already had a machine-gun officer. Back I came to my unit with my tail between my legs but a determination to try yet another unit. A month later the Oxford and Bucks Light Infantry went over to France, straight up to the front line and had severe casualties against overwhelming German odds. I had a lucky escape. I applied next to the Twentieth Battalion of the London Regiment (Blackheath and Woolwich) T.A. which was attached to the Royal West Kent Regiment. I was accepted. The amoeba blossomed into a pink-faced, full-blown second lieutenant, complete with smart uniform, polished Sam Browne belt and revolver. I was rising twenty and, in my own estimation, Napoleon was about to be eclipsed.

Meanwhile the machine-gun vision came true. I was picked to set up a machine-gun course for the whole brigade. This took some months. During that time the First Battalion which was in France suffered appalling casualties especially at the Battle of Loos. A young officers' life in those days averaged three weeks only, when he reached the front line of battle. They were picked off like flies by German snipers who were deadly.

We sent out draft after draft of officers who lived for less than a month. The machine-gun corps, luckily for me, kept me busy at home. Then came my turn. I was posted to the First Battalion in the Loos sector. At last I could hear the guns.

For the next two years we were on continuous active service, in and out of the trenches, more often in than out, on the hottest parts of the Western Front including Ypres, Passchendaele, Vimy Ridge, Souchez and the Somme. One saw and suffered pretty well all the worst horrors of trench warfare. Enough has been written about them. We saw wounded men eaten by rats which swarmed. They were man-eaters. We lost comrades drowned alive in liquid mud. Others were buried alive in trenches and dug-outs which were either wrecked by shell-fire or blown up by German engineers driving tunnels under them, packed with explosive. All this, coupled with bayonet attacks in the dark hours when one went 'over the top' into a grim world of mud, shell-holes, barbed-wire entanglements and scattered corpses, to be mown down by machine-gun fire, blown to bits by bombs or shelled mercilessly by barrages which seemed to rend the very earth. This we all suffered.

The highlights stand out, some tragic, some amusing. There was the afternoon order to go 'over the top' when our men, grim-faced, bayonets fixed climbed out of their muddy trench on the Somme and charged the German lines. A creeping barrage of our artillery had already destroyed most of the enemy barbed-wire entanglements. Suddenly, out of a deep dug-out directly in front of the ground over which my company had to charge, there emerged three German machine-gun teams. They went into instant action. Their rapid fire swept the whole of our front. Our men went down like shot rabbits. Luckily there was much cover in the shape of shell-holes, half full of water. Into these we tumbled, lay flat, and fired back. I ordered my company to keep down and keep shooting. The withering machine-gun fire would have killed every man jack of them. I knew that behind us, coming up in support, was a new-fangled thing called a tank. We had not yet seen one. The tank or tanks might arrive within minutes, hours or days. We lay, muddy and sodden, in our shell-holes hoping for the new wonder to materialize.

Suddenly, with a hideous clanking, an iron-clad vehicle, perhaps fifteen feet long, mounted on caterpillar tracks with a couple of small guns firing from side turrets, lumbered up behind us, bumping and wallowing over the shell-holes. The three teams of German machine-gunners poured their united fire into it. The tank lumbered straight at them. As it advanced, towering above them, the Germans vanished down their deep dug-out like trapped rabbits. The tank rocked to and fro over the entrance to the dug-out. The walls caved in. A shower of earth and wooden supports cascaded on the men below. Ruthlessly, the tank pounded them into their living grave. Then it settled down flat on top of what had been the entrance to the dug-out and stayed. Those German machine-gunners were buried alive. The officer commanding the tank and his small crew got out and came back to us, having destroyed all the vital instruments aboard the tank which was completely out of action. This was only the second day on which tanks had gone into action in France. I remember that officer's face as one remembers the face of the man who has saved you from death.

Two years later when I was convalescing from wounds in a tiny hospital with only eight patients in a house at Bournemouth, who should join us but that young tank captain!

Having disposed of the three invincible machine-gun teams the rest of my company advanced, through the grounds of an old abbey. There we set up a strong-point. I counted our losses. The company had 'gone over the top' nearly two hundred strong with five officers. One of them was a mere boy, straight from Sandhurst. He had reported to me in the trench the night before with a smart parade-ground salute. I told him, a little testily, that it was no time or place for the usual formalities. I sent him off to find a sergeant who would take him in charge and give him practical advice. I was too busy planning the attack, which was imminent.

When, in the abbey grounds, I counted the losses, there were only sixty-eight men left alive out of nearly two hundred and, apart from myself, only one officer out of five. That survivor was the boy from Sandhurst. It was his first night and day in the trenches.

We dug in and sat tight in our strong-point. We had lost touch with the battalion H.Q. For all I knew we might well have been isolated with Germans in front of us and Germans behind. Two days later the Australians joined us on our right flank. Our left flank was 'in the air'.

Suddenly, in the October afternoon mist, German soldiers loomed up *behind us*, twenty or thirty of them. They had been hiding in the cellars of the abbey and were not aware of our existence. It was not the time or place to take prisoners. We could not have held them or sent them back to base. So we shot them down. That is war.

Ahead of us in a field of long grass a solitary German soldier suddenly rose to his feet. He had been hiding in the grass and had lost his belt. He started to run, desperately holding up his trousers with both hands. It was such comic relief that I hadn't the heart to shoot him. We let him go.

Next day the London Irish counter-attacked on our left flank and joined with us. At last our front line was intact. For this little effort in capturing and holding our strong-point I was awarded the Military Cross.* In turn I recommended 2nd Lieutenant Steel, the Sandhurst boy who did so splendidly in his first attack. He also got the M.C.

More comic relief at Souchez off the tail-end of Vimy Ridge. There we took over a line of shattered trenches which had been occupied by the French. The trenches had been blown to bits. There was little or no cover for our men. Corps Command ordered us not to fire on the Germans or provoke them in any way until we had re-dug our trenches and fortified ourselves in the proper manner. It was going to be a long job. We had to lie low, fire no shot and get to work with shovels, pick-axes and trenching tools. Peace reigned between the German lines and our own.

Imagine my surprise therefore when, later that night in the twilight, three German officers suddenly loomed up on the edge of the trench a few yards from us. I gazed at them in blank surprise. I did not even reach for my revolver. One of them spoke up in English: 'We did not know you English were here. We thought you were the French. You onderstand zat we come every night to have dinner with ze French officers.'

Bearing in mind my instructions neither to shoot nor provoke the Germans, I replied coolly: 'You are welcome to stay and have dinner if you wish. But I must warn you you will not go

* The Official comment was: The tanks later silenced these machine guns. The position was most successfully held by troops under Lt. Needham who held on under most difficult conditions until our line was established round Eaucourt l'Abbaye.

back. You will stay as prisoners. Will you dine – or return?'

'Ach! I tank you. We go back to our lines.' And he and his companions saluted me, turned on their heels and marched off.

This extraordinary situation had an almost unbelievable follow-up. Next day our men were out in no-man's land repairing the barbed-wire entanglements which had been blasted to shreds. The Germans were repairing theirs. Neither side fired on the other. So we struck up a conversation. They told us that they were Saxons and were undergoing 'Kaiser's punishment' because they had mutinied against being sent into the holocaust of the Battle of Verdun. 'Kaisers' punishment' meant that they were condemned to a full month in the trenches without relief. They had decided therefore that, instead of having a full month of constant fighting, they would make it a month of unofficial armistice.

So we ended up by borrowing some of their mallets and other tools with which we mended our own barbed-wire fences. In return we gave them tins of apple-and-plum jam.

I reported this extraordinary situation to battalion H.Q. who passed it on to corps H.Q. They promptly sent us a supply of propaganda newspapers and leaflets printed in German which we dutifully delivered to our new friend-enemies. They received them with smiles and abrupt little bows and devoured them. This little idyll went on for a week or ten days.

Then, on a dark night, without warning, all hell broke loose. A thunderous artillery barrage rent the sky, blasted the earth and played hell with men, trenches and wire. Heavy shells sent up fountains of earth. Star-shells lit the sky. Minenwerfers or flying mines which our men called 'toffee apples' or 'minnies' came bumbling over, burst and shook the ground. The idyll was at an end. The friendly Saxons had been withdrawn and the Prussian Guard had taken over.

Twenty-four hours before this battle started my jinx or protective fairy had been at it again. I contracted trench fever, the result of being bitten badly by lice which were thick as bees in the dirty French trenches.* The result was a temperature of 104

---

* It was eventually established that lice were the agent which spread trench fever.

and a head which throbbed like a brass gong. I was half-stupefied with pain and was packed off to the field hospital well in the rear, where I was put to bed and told to stay. That night the sky was shattered by the artillery barrage on my company. I struggled out of bed, got my trousers on and was about to go back to my men. There was nothing heroic about this. In war officers and men are closely knit together. One's instinct is to be with them when they are in a tight spot. It was the natural thing to do. This was squashed by the medical officer who said brutally; 'You'll be a liability to them, not an asset. With a temperature of 104 you'll be a menace. Back to bed.'

Soon after, the battalion, which had taken a fearful mauling, was ordered back to the rear for a long rest. Then we were marched off, completely re-equipped for the Somme. Every man knew that he was potential cannon-fodder. Three-quarters of our original strength had been killed. Any one of us might be the next to go. Yet, on that long march through bright harvest fields and orchards full of glowing fruit, with peace and beauty all about us, but with death waiting round the corner, the men sang like larks and joked the eternal soldiers' jokes.

We were reinforced by many new drafts. The grim horrors of trench warfare lost nothing when they were retold to the newcomers. We were three weeks marching through the lush beauties of Picardy whose fields rang with that immortal song, 'Roses are Blooming in Picardy', from lusty throats. Then came Albert, on the Somme, where we were to camp. Back to the horrors of the battlefield. We saw, high above the shell-shattered streets of that fine old medieval town, that most extraordinary religious symbol of the whole Western Front, the statue of the Virgin bearing in her arms the Infant Jesus, hanging precariously from the tall shell-torn steeple of the church as though she was offering the Holy Infant as a sign of peace to come to the people below. That, I think, made an impression on all of us.

One episode on the Somme stands out vividly. After violent fighting in which we suffered heavy losses the battalion was sent behind the lines to rest in bivouacs in orchards. The general arrived on a horse accompanied by his A.D.C. and his galloper. He reined in his horse and declaimed in a ringing voice: 'Well done my boys. You've shown the good old Cockney spirit.' He then went to see the colonel. Half an hour later the colonel sent for the officers. We found him in tears.

'The general has said that we must go into the attack again, at once, to clean up a few places here and there, as he puts it,' the colonel announced. 'I told him point-blank that my officers and men were so shell-shocked and exhausted that they were not fit to fight. I told him that if you were ordered back into battle I should refuse to take responsibility and it would rest squarely on him. You are staying here.' That was the end of the general, as far as we were concerned.

Night patrols into the eerie mystery and lurking death of no man's land were the most macabre exercises of the war. No man's land, as all old soldiers know, was that strip of hideous territory, pitted with shell holes, smothered with debris of bully-beef tins, rusty wire and the other off-scourings of war, including shattered human bodies, which lay between the German lines and our own. No man's land could be anything in width from 50 yards to two or three hundred yards. To venture there in day-time was to court certain death. One would not have gone five yards without getting a bullet from a German sniper.

Night patrols went out in utter secrecy and dead silence to find out, if possible, the strength and the disposition of the opposing forces. If you were lucky you might capture a stray German soldier from his own trenches or wiring-party, who would be brought back as a prisoner so that we could determine from his uniform and questioning, the name and, if possible, the numbers of the regiment opposing us.

Each night patrol consisted of about eight men including a junior officer and a sergeant. They had to crawl out of the trench over the parapet of sandbags and then worm their way on hands and knees, often in deep mud, by a zig-zag passage or tunnel through our own barbed-wire defences which were several yards wide – an impassable tangle. Once through the wire, it was possible to breathe gently, pray – and how one did pray – and move forward on hands and knees into the unknown.

Having sent out a number of patrols I decided it was time that I, as the man in command, should take my own share of the risk.

The company commander was not supposed to do this, but it seemed to me essential that one should know and understand the full risk.

Never shall I forget the chilling feeling of utter loneliness which struck me as we crawled out of our tunnel through the barbed wire, deployed ourselves and crawled forward on hands and knees through stinking mud and every other sort of hazard towards the enemy lines. When my boot rattled a rusty bully-beef tin I shuddered. Great grey rats, which fed on the dead, scampered almost under one's nose. They were as big as small cats. One knew that the slightest sound would bring a burst of machine-gun fire from the German trenches, followed by a grenade or two. Then the star-shells went up, glittering into the sky, to burst like fireworks and shed a ghastly, dancing, momentary light over the whole blood-curdling scene. Then one lay as flat as a pancake.

At one place no man's land was only thirty yards wide. I estimated that on one patrol we were within five to ten yards of the Germans whom we could hear speaking perfectly plainly. You would think that no one would choose willingly to go into no man's land.

Yet there was a crazy hero in my own regiment, one Captain Elliott, who made a positive hobby of it. Night after night he went out *on his own*. He would be out for as long as an hour, crawling like a worm from our front line to the German front line. He spoke fluent German and would lie doggo in the mud a few yards from the lip of the enemy trenches listening to the conversation and making careful mental notes. One night he actually slipped into the German trenches at a point where they were sparsely manned and hid himself in a traverse in the German line where he got an earful of news. This was too good to last. There came the night when Captain Elliott, the bravest and foolhardiest man I knew, came back to our trenches with his hair parted. He had a thick shock of it. A German bullet had not only parted it neatly but laid open a bleeding furrow through the skin of his scalp. Had it been a quarter of an inch lower he would have been dead. This dampened even Captain Elliott. He was never again quite the same light-hearted night walker.

Then came the most frightening and shattering episode of the whole war – the blowing up of Hill 60. It was probably the greatest single explosion in a war which was, in essence, a long series of almost continuous explosions. When Hill 60 was blown sky-high a mighty fountain of earth and human bodies literally darkened the sky for a few seconds. Friends who were in camp at Aldershot at that time told me afterwards that although they frequently heard the thunder of gunfire in France, when Hill 60 went up, the Hampshire earth shook beneath their feet and a long shuddering boom made the air quiver. Those soldiers at home in England wondered what on earth – or under the earth – had happened.

Hill 60 was no hill but a mere eminence not fifty feet high in the flat lands of the Ypres Salient. It was held by the Germans. Our sappers were ordered to drive a series of tunnels under it, pack them with high explosives and blow the lot to blazes. It sounds easy until you try to do it. Our sappers were Durham miners who had been drafted to the Royal Engineers. They were first cousins to moles. They could undermine anything. The Germans had their own human moles, coalminers in uniform. They too were busy burrowing.

Our sappers, digging night and day, with pickaxes and shovels, could hear the Germans digging away at close range. It was a toss-up who got under the centre of the hill first. The Germans with the military cunning of their race tried to fox us by installing automatic picks which went on chopping away when their men were withdrawn from the tunnel. At any moment either side might withdraw its miners, having packed the tunnels with a devasting load of explosive and fire the lot. By the grace of God our sappers got there first. The fuses were set and we in the trenches, not two hundred yards away, were told to take cover.

A moment or two later the earth seemed to open. The shattering roar stunned us. Speech and thought were paralysed for minutes. The sky was darkened by a cloud of earth, dust, flying bodies, pit-props and general debris. It descended on us in a black avalanche. Many of our men were temporarily half-buried.

The earth was still shaking when we received the order to go 'over the top' with fixed bayonets. We scrambled out of our trenches, white-faced and still shaking from that fearful blast, and charged across the sodden, quaking ground. The object was to capture immediately a commanding position overlooking the vast crater which had just been made by the explosion. We dug ourselves into hastily made trenches using trenching tools, and mounted our machine-guns and promptly had a commanding field of fire across the whole width of the crater. By the time we had consolidated our position I doubt if we had gained more than a hundred yards of enemy territory. That is the sort of war it was – something utterly different from the fast-moving campaigns of the Second World War. Once you were stuck in the Flanders mud, whether you were English, French or German you were stuck for good. Only a major artillery barrage of earth-shattering magnitude could breach either front line. The generals were not to blame. It was simply a case of sticking it out until the moral of either side finally cracked.

One of the worst aspects of that war, was, as I have mentioned, the hideous menace of the giant man-eating rats. They would not hesitate to attack and eat a badly wounded man if he was left lying out in no man's land on a dark night. These rats which in normal circumstances were no more than common field-rats of ordinary size, grew to an abnormal size and a tigerish ferocity on a diet of human flesh.

At the back of our line was an extra-large dug-out. This we used as a mortuary to hold the bodies of our dead comrades until they could be removed to back areas and properly buried in military cemeteries. Day and night two sentries were posted in that dug-out to keep the rats at bay. They were armed with heavy sticks. We, the officers, became crack revolver shots simply because we had endless practice in shooting rats.

During that war almost every form of devilish warfare was employed from tanks to mustard gas and liquid fire. Mustard gas burnt out the lungs. Liquid fire burned men alive. There were incessant trench raids, constant artillery barrages, in which every sort of shell from the thunderous 'Jack Johnson' to the prestiferous little 'whizz-bang' was used. Every now and then an unseen stupendous missile thundered high over us in the upper air towards the back of the German lines. It went over like an express train. These were the sixteen-inch shells fired from great naval guns outside Paris.

At Ypres I met my own Waterloo. I was standing by a sand-bagged shelter, well above ground, musing on the fallibility of mankind, when a German 'whizz-bang', an 18-pounder shell to wit, burst on the other side of the sandbagged wall. Up it went and down I went. Most of the wall of sand and earth descended on me and partly buried me. I struggled out like a half-trapped rabbit and stood up dizzily. The world for a few minutes was very shaky.

The colonel heard of it and sent for me. He asked, 'How long have you been in France, Needham?' I said, 'Getting on for two years, sir.' He said, 'Well, I think you are getting a bit tired. You've had a long spell and I don't think you should gamble with your luck any longer. Take a month's leave in England, enjoy yourself and try to forget the war. And at the end of your leave I will arrange for you to have a medical examination in England.' Home I went to London. By the end of the month I had my medical examination. The board were very sympathetic and directed, 'You'd better stay here.' So ended my war.

CHAPTER THREE

The Genius Who Was Northcliffe

Back to Fleet Street – I join the *Daily Mail* – 'Feared, Respected and Burnt on the Stock Exchange' – Northcliffe's 'Grand Manner' – The Epic of Mr Imber – 'Get Yourself a Rolls-Royce' – 'Lord Imber' – And His Dramatic Downfall – The Hall Porter Is Promoted in His Place – Northcliffe's Final Dementia – Genius of the Harmsworths

Back in England I was invited to go on a lecture tour of America where I was supposed to stand on platforms in uniform and tell audiences how brave we had all been. That was not my cup of tea. I declined.

One thing which annoyed me intensely was the ignorant clamour set up by a lot of old women and well-meaning teetotallers who said it was criminal to serve a rum ration to young soldiers in the trenches. One's mind went back to damp, grey mornings of half-light when men and officers in sodden clothing and often in pouring rain, stood-to on the fire-step of front-line trenches gazing silently, impassively, into no man's land. If there was no shell-fire the silence was intense. Not a man spoke. No laughter. No jokes. Perhaps the chatter of teeth in half-frozen mouths. Then, far-down the line, the rum ration started on its travels from hand to hand in a great stone jar. It acted like magic. One heard jokes and comfortable talk as that precious spirit, rich in molasses, brought warmth and light to men half-frozen and half-dead. They were ready to fight again.

The virtue of rum was explained by the M.O. 'Give a man brandy,' he said, 'and it may turn him into a hero, but it quickens the action of his heart. If he is wounded the accelerated heart will pump the blood more quickly from his wound. Whisky, when the first warmth has worn off, leaves him cold. Gin is depressive. Rum is rich in sugar. It slows the heart, warms the blood and thickens it. It may prevent fatal loss of blood. Your wounded man has a double chance of recovery.'

After a spell of war service at home I was demobilized. Back to Fleet Street I went, via a brief and thorny spell on the

The nowadays unrecognisably athletic figure on the left is the author being congratulated by a fellow officer outside Buckingham Palace after the award of the Military Cross

Above: Lord Northcliffe, the man who made modern Fleet Street, in a typically Napoleonic pose. *Below:* Lord Castlerosse writing at his desk. In writing the words 'To "Sweet William"' he forgot that 'sweet William' is a fisherman's name for a voracious sea-fish

staff of *Tit-Bits* under a man I neither liked nor respected. I had my eye on bigger game and wider fields of action. I got a job on the *Evening News* and soon came in contact with Lord Northcliffe.

Northcliffe was then one of the most powerful men in England. He could make or break governments. His *Daily Mail* was feared, respected and hated. It had been burned publicly on the Stock Exchange. Northcliffe cared nothing for public opinion since he was convinced that he could mould that opinion. For the first time in my life I met a true giant of the printed word.

This extraordinary man had done a very good job in the war. The Germans struck a Medal of Hate against him for the work he did at that time in the field of anti-German propaganda. As a young man on the *Evening News* he was at first only a name to me, but naturally gossip and stories flooded in concerning the greatness of this man. Everything he did was in the grand manner. I remember the party he gave on the fiftieth anniversary of the *Daily Mail* which was organized on such a scale that only Olympia could hold the guests. Parade-ground memories were stirred when I saw hundreds of 'nippies' (Lyons teashop waitresses) 'dressing by the right' to their stations of serving. Any general would have been proud of their disciplined array. There I had my first glimpse of Northcliffe.

He was of medium height, square shouldered, heavily built, clean shaven with a bull-dog jaw, piercing eyes set well apart, a strong nose and a heavy hank of hair brushed over the left-hand side of his forehead, rather as Hitler brushed his hair. He had an air of power and command, which was softened by his Irish charm and manner. I next saw him at the Ideal Home Exhibition at Olympia. He was striding through the Great Hall, appraising the exhibits, with his Advertising Manager, Wareham-Smith. Suddenly he spotted a dignified gentleman in black coat and vest with striped trousers, a stock tie and an eye-glass. He was white-haired with black bushy eyebrows. A very distinguished-looking man.

'I know that man,' Northcliffe exclaimed, and strode over to him.

'How do you do, sir. What do you think of the show?' The dignified man replied, 'I think it is a splendid show, sir.' Northcliffe said, 'Thank you very much. You've encouraged me.'

He returned to Wareham-Smith and said, 'I can't think of that chap's name. I've met him before. Who is he?'

'He's one of your advertising canvassers on the *Daily Mail*,' Wareham-Smith replied. 'And his name is Imber.'

I owed my introduction to the Northcliffe empire to this Mr Imber. I met him first on the Hendon Golf Course. As usual, he was well-dressed, dignified and striking. I asked him to play golf. We struck up an acquaintanceship. I felt honoured when he invited me back to his house in Finchley to dine. There he had three pretty daughters. I got the impression that he thought I might be a suitable companion for one of them. I had by this time discovered that he was the Advertisement Manager of the *Evening News*, having climbed the ladder from canvassing. I had my eye on him as the possible key to a job on the *Evening News* rather than an eye on the daughters since I was already engaged.

He was sympathetic concerning my difficulties with *Tit-Bits*. To my delight he said, 'You must come with me.' The result was a job as an advertising sales representative at the rate of £500 a year – equal to £2,000 or more today – on October 22nd, 1920. It was my first real job in Fleet Street.

Imber swiftly made his mark as an advertising manager of the first order. He packed the paper with advertisements. The repercussion from Northcliffe was astonishing. One morning before Imber left his home in Finchley for the office, Northcliffe was on the telephone.

'Imber, you're spoiling my newspaper. It's packed with far too many advertisements.'

'That's what I'm paid to do, chief,' the astonished Imber replied.

'Never mind,' Northcliffe replied, 'I want to talk to you. I leave for Pau in France this morning. Meet me at Victoria Station.'

Northcliffe hustled Imber on to the train with him. They

travelled down to Dover together. Imber, a clever man and an opportunist, rightly saw his chance. He told his chief that he wanted to widen the advertising field, to capture the princes of industry, to get the big names to advertise in 'our newspapers'. Northcliffe saw the vision in a flash.

'Have you a motor-car?'

'Yes, sir, an Armstrong-Siddeley.'

'Not good enough. Order yourself a Rolls-Royce and charge it to the Company. You look the sort of man who should ride in a Rolls-Royce. Have you a wife?'

'Yes, sir.'

'Is she good-looking? Does she dress well?'

'Yes, chief.'

'Then send her to Worth. Tell her to order the best day and evening outfits. Charge them to my Company. Then go on a tour of big business. Take your wife with you. Take the best suite in the best hotel in every town you visit. But before you go, give me a list of all these big men in industry. I will write personally to each one and ask him to be good enough to meet you and to listen to you. You and your wife will entertain them in your suite and no expense spared.'

Imber came straight back to London from Dover, ordered a Rolls on his way to the office and then walked into the *Daily Mail* building and told the top brass what he had done. There was uproar. Jealousy was rampant. Imber was the most disliked man of the moment. None the less the plan went ahead. Northcliffe sent the personal letters. The tour went ahead. It pulled in the business. Imber went from strength to strength. In Northcliffe's eyes he could do no wrong.

It was Northcliffe's practice to send daily bulletins to his higher executives. Before long came a paralysing bulletin that announced that 'this wonder-man Imber' was to be known by the staff in future as 'Lord Imber'. Northcliffe went on to say that Imber's distinguished dress and bearing could never be mistaken for that of anyone other than a lord. 'In fact,' he added, 'I have instructed my personal staff never to refer to him otherwise than as Lord Imber.' You can imagine the reaction of rage, amusement, envy, hatred, malice and all uncharitableness which this excited among the executives from the Directors down. Mr Imber was not popular.

Imber pursued his impassive, decorous, but opportunistic way. He never missed a chance.

I had by this time been appointed Advertisement Manager of the *Evening News*, Imber had a certain friendship for me born of our meetings on the Hendon Golf Course and at his house, and confided in me. I heard the full tale of 'Lord Imber'.

Not long afterwards came the anti-climax. Few, if any of us, knew at the time that Lord Northcliffe was becoming mentally deranged. The first, incipient signs of the disease which killed him a year or so later, began to make themselves felt by his extraordinary eccentricities. He behaved like a Roman emperor. His attitude to his favourite, Imber, changed drastically. A bulletin announced that the title of 'Lord Imber' was to be dropped. Executives were directed to refer to him in future as 'that man Imber'. Poor Horace Imber took this devastating attack badly. He was cast-down. He looked a hunted man. Then came a worse broadside in a further bulletin. Northcliffe announced: 'I must warn this man Imber that I am very dissatisfied with his work and I suggest that he takes heed of my words because I am most unhappy and dissatisfied.' Came a third bulletin to the effect that the hall porter, Mr Glover, was to be appointed to take the place of Mr Imber. Glover, incidentally, stood about six foot six inches in height and had not an aitch to his name. A further bulletin waspishly announced: 'I understand that the appointment of Mr Glover to take the place of Imber is being taken as a joke. Therefore I would like Mr Glover to attend at my house in Carlton Gardens at 3 o'clock tomorrow afternoon. I would ask the Advertising Department to attend at 3.15, including Imber.'

We all turned up at the great Northcliffe mansion overlooking St James's Park. We were ushered into the music room, a stately apartment, and seated on rows of gilt chairs. The air of expectancy was dramatic. One felt infinitely sorry for the wretched Horace Imber sitting pale, alone and shunned.

Precisely at 3.15 a footman flung open the door. Lord

Northcliffe marched in, followed by the towering Mr Glover in a blue serge suit with his hair slicked back with hair oil, smoking a large cigar with the band on. It was the first time I had ever seen him out of commissionaire's uniform. We all stood up, and were then commanded to sit down. Glover remained standing, fumbling with his cigar.

He looked the Cockney that he was. When on duty at the office he wore a band on his arm which proclaimed INTER-PRETER. His French was not that of the Quai d'Orsay. Lord Northcliffe said, 'I want you to listen to Mr Glover. Mr Glover is a highly intelligent man. He speaks many languages. I have just been having a chat with him.' Northcliffe did not announce the languages to which he referred. They were, one guessed, non-existent. Then Glover made his speech. It was to this effect:

'The chief' as done the signal honner hof happointin' me,' he paused (I held my breath. This was the most astonishing moment of my newspaper career. What was Glover going to say?) then, with much dignity, he added, 'the Art Critic of the Advertising Department. 'E 'opes as 'ow I shall 'ave the full support of yew gennlemen.' The audience was stunned. Poor Imber seemed to wince to half his normal size.

That was the end of the drama. Lord Northcliffe then held a sort of seminar of questions and answers with the young men of the various advertising departments. Everyone who wished to make his mark with the chief, and there were many, got up and asid his little piece. All except Mr Coggins, the Classified Advertisement Manager. He seemed supremely bored. He gazed at the pictures on the walls. He studied the ceiling. He looked out of the windows. Lord Northcliffe looked point blank at him.

'You, sir,' he suddenly demanded, 'What have you to say concerning the question put by the last speaker?'

'I er – Im' afraid I didnt' hear it, chief, 'the wretched Coggins blurted out. As a matter of fact, sir, I'm a little hard of hearing.'

Northcliffe asked, 'Are you deaf?' to which the reply was, 'Slightly, sir.' Do you use the telephone?' Northcliffe demanded.

Coggins, delighted at being brought into the picture replied, 'I use it a lot, chief. The telephone is a vital part of my job. I do half my business on the phone.'

Northcliffe snapped, 'Mr Coggins, I order you never to use the telephone again. There is nothing more annoying than to speak on the telephone to a man at the other end who can't hear what one is saying.'

The wretched Coggins went back to his office handicapped beyond the dreams of torture. He scarcely dared lift the telephone lest the voice at the other end should be that of Northcliffe.

Thereafter Northcliffe's oddities of behaviour became even more pronounced. The Emperor Caligula who appointed his horse a Pro-Consul of Rome was almost outdone by the appointment of Glover.

Next morning Glover was on duty as usual at the front door of Carmelite House. In walked Milliken, the Advertisement Manager of the *Daily Mail*. Glover greeted him with the words: 'Mr Milliken, the Chief and Hi think that the hadvertisements on page three are a bit too much on the e'avy side.'

'Go and stuff yourself,' snapped Milliken and vanished upstairs.

Finally the Directors decided to issue a writ for libel against Northcliffe. Every Director except one put his name to it. The one man who abstained out of sheer loyalty to his chief was Horace Imber.

Soon after he went. Whether he was fired or forced to resign I do not know. All I do know is that his departure was not of his own seeking. He took an inferior job at less pay with another newspaper. Soon after he died. So ended an unique personal chapter in the tempestuous story of Northcliffe.

The sun of Northcliffe had not yet set below the horizon of Fleet Street before a new orb – or should it be firework – arose in the West. Its name was William Maxwell Aitken. He was to make as great an impact on Fleet Street and on national affairs as did Northcliffe. In many ways his personal impact was greater since he took a leading part more than once in the affairs of government and was an outstanding Minister of Aviation during the Second World War.

The Harmsworth family, until the arrival of Aitken from

Canada, had been the great Press lords. Northcliffe had created an empire of news, propaganda and publicity which was unique. Born of a line of Irish parsons with an Irish mother and a father who was an English barrister-at-law, his background epitomized that of the sober middle-classes who are the backbone of the country. He and his brothers achieved that Valhalla of the middle classes – hereditary honours. Northcliffe and his brother Harold both became viscounts: Viscount Northcliffe and Viscount Rothermere. Leicester Harmsworth became a baronet, so did another brother. Three of them were millionaires. They acquired and still own immensely valuable real-estate in the Fleet Street area. They bought landed estates complete with stately homes. Their descendants today are sober peers and baronets. Northcliffe left no heir. The rest of the Harmsworth clan pursue their highly respectable social and financial paths. They will, I am sure, forgive me if I say that although Northcliffe was an undoubted journalistic genius and his brother, the first Lord Rothermere, equally an undoubted financial genius, their descendants have shown little of the creative flair which made the family fortunes.

There is an old saying among farmers that 'the masters' foot is the best dung on the land'. Northcliffe epitomized this by his constant day-by-day minute-by-minute direction of his news-papers. Not a line of print escaped his eye. His mind bubbled with inspiration, suggestion, direction and command. Hence the rise to power of the *Daily Mail* and the *Evening News*. The *Daily Mail* in its heyday was as great a power in English poli-tics and as profound an influence on everyday English thought as *The Times* had been under the editorship of the great Delane when it was nicknamed 'The Thunderer'. The *Daily Mail* became the new Thunderer under the editorship of such great journalists as Fish and Marlow. *The Times* deflated its thunder to the pon-tifical wheeze of an elderly, pompous clubman. It let the *Daily Mail* clamour from the rooftops.

Today whilst the present Lord Rothermere, an amiable and a charming man, is busy with his stately country house and his equally stately town house, Warwick House in the purlieus of St James's Palace, the *Daily Mail,* alas, declines in substance and importance. As well, it has changed its appearance, from that of a national newspaper to the format of a provincial tabloid. It no longer has its former magic of inspiration.

Meanwhile the *Evening News,* with the greatest circulation of any evening paper in the world, has in the last year or so changed its tone from that of a cosy, readable family newspaper beloved by the Londoner, the suburban strap-hanger and the provincial housewife to that of a clinical, impersonal news-sheet. A sad state of affairs when one reflects that in my youth there were at least half a dozen London evening newspapers. The *Globe, Pall Mall Gazette,* the *Westminster Gazette, The Star, Evening News* and *Evening Standard.* The last two alone remain.

One wonders how much longer the Harmsworth newspaper empire will survive, in London at least. Its great chain of provincial newspapers may well weather the storms of today. I have a particular affection for the *Evening News* since I was Advertisement Manager of that newspaper during the inspiring editorship of Fitzhugh who was followed by that equally capable and beloved journalist C. Reginald Willis, a man who had the rare knack of sensing the warm personality of his readers. He indeed made it 'the Cockney's family evening paper'.

I had a second personal link with the *Evening News.* Lord Northcliffe had a godson. His name was Alfred Pemberton. He was the son of that famous journalist and author, Sir Max Pemberton, one of the great literary stars in the *Daily Mail* firmament. Northcliffe was very fond of his godson Alfred, who, after all, took his Christian name from Northcliffe. The godson became in due course the Advertisement Manager of the *Evening News* having previously been in the Advertising Department of *The Times* which Northcliffe had bought from the Walter family. It was a nerve-shaking change from the stately decorum of Printing House Square to vortex of highly charged activity at Carmelite House. The change was too violent. Alfred Pemberton soon betook himself to the even statelier atmosphere of *The Tatler,* which under the editorship of Teddy Huskinson was then the leading glossy snob journal of Society.

He had many rich and influential friends in business and in Society. Some of them persuaded him that a glowing future awaited him if he would set up in business on his own as an advertising agent. He did so. The result in a very short time was one of the most prosperous advertising agencies in London, housed in a stately home in Park Lane. Today my friend 'Pem' pursues his stately way as to the ducal manner born.

When Horace Imber left the *Daily Mail* he left in my own mind and heart a chill void. I had lost a good friend, the man who set my foot on the first rung of the Fleet Street ladder. The warmth went out of one's business life.

CHAPTER FOUR

The Beaverbrook Era

I Join the Most Remarkable Man Fleet Street Has Ever Known –
'Power and Genius' – How He Bought the *Daily Express* – Rat-Ridden
Offices – The Great R.D.B. – The General Strike Hits Britain – And Is
Smashed – 'Cavalry Charge' Down Ludgate Hill – Lady Louis Mount-
batten as 'Phone Girl' – The Undoing of Sir Beverley Baxter – £10,000
a Year for a Publican-Cartoonist – S. N. Alexander, the City Genius
– 'Who Was Your Father?'

In the spring of 1926 a week or so before the General Strike
semi-paralysed Britain my wagon was hitched to a star. I did not
do the hitching. Nor did I seek the star. The star which domi-
nated the brilliant firmament of Fleet Street and the wider sky
of Britain and her Empire sent a lesser star earthward to hitch
me on.

In short, Lord Beaverbrook sent for me. I was then Advertisement Manager of the *Evening News*, a good enough job for
most men. But inwardly I was not happy. I had lost my friend,
Horace Imber. His death left me unsettled. Out of the blue came
a telephone call from a remarkable New Zealander named
Freddie Doidge, General Manager of the *Sunday Express*. It
was then a new paper fighting hard to make its mark in the cut-
throat jungle of Fleet Street. It was the first newspaper that
Beaverbrook had launched personally. Therefore it was his pet,
his pride and his joy.

Doidge, tall and saturnine, was completely unknown to me.
He told me on the telephone that he would be glad if I could
meet him at Anderton's Hotel in Fleet Street to discuss a matter
of the utmost secrecy. He enhanced the Edgar Wallace atmosphere of cloak and dagger mystery by saying: 'For the purpose
of arranging our interview, you will be known as Mr Brown and
I shall be Mr Clark.' Since Andertons' Hotel was the very hub
of Fleet Street it was a hundred to one that both of us would be
spotted and identified by any of a score of newspapermen who
might be in the place. Nonetheless Clark and Brown it was. He
came straight to the point. Would I like to leave the *Evening
News* and become Advertisement Manager of the *Sunday Ex-*

press? The offer staggered me and also disappointed me. I considered that to leave a well-paid executive job on the most successful evening paper in Britain with the largest evening circulation in the world for a new weekly which I had not actually either seen or read would be a downhill step and a great risk. I said so, bluntly.

Doidge painted a rosy picture of success to come. He emphasized the fact, which all the world knew, that Beaverbrook was the new driving force in Fleet Street, a man of exceptional vision, energy, power and genius. This was precisely the atmosphere of personal magnetism and inspiration which I had lost when Northcliffe died. That fact alone decided me to take the new job with all the risks it entailed. I did not say as much to Doidge. I drove the hardest bargain I could – and got it. Thus started an unbroken career of forty-five years in close partnership with the most remarkable man that Fleet Street has ever known.

William Maxwell Aitken, first Baron Beaverbrook, was remarkable. He began life as the son of a poor Presbyterian minister in a small township in the wooded wilds of New Brunswick, Canada. He was of pioneering stock and inherited the pioneers' attitude towards life. He made a fortune counted in millions of dollars before he was thirty. He came to this country in about 1910 to try his hand at politics. He had a Canadian accent which many people found difficult to understand. In his early days in this country before the First World War he was conspicuous as the exception to the rules of impeccable dress and behaviour. In a world of top-hats, frock-coats and striped trousers he dressed carelessly, had a shock of tousled hair, asked outrageously direct questions, laid down the law to his elders and betters and blazed with fervour for the British Empire. He was an Imperialist who wagged the flag with both hands and preached the Gospel of Empire with a harsh Canadian accent and a splendid choice of Biblical parables, texts and phrases.

He made his first mark in public life when he won Ashton-under-Lyne for the Tory Party. It was a Liberal stronghold. He attacked it with ferocity. He canvassed from house to house preaching his doctrine of Empire Free Trade with blazing eloquence. His face in repose could look cold, forbidding and down-right ugly. He had a low brow, beetling eyebrows, cold grey eyes, thick lips, a wide mouth, squat nose and high cheekbones. He was nobody's pin-up boy. But when he smiled the ugly face lit up with a warmth and charm which captured men and captivated women. There has never been a man quite like him.

Whatever he put his mind to, he mastered. He had a fantastic gift for assimilating facts, figures and statistics. He could rattle them off like a machine-gun. Transcending this encyclopaedic knowledge was his super-human foresight, inventiveness and invincible drive to succeed. He let nothing and no one bar his path. He could be ruthless to a degree. But he was always fair. Little-minded men feared and hated him. They slandered him behind his back and fawned upon him to his face. The ordinary man recognised on sight that here was a real genius. A man of immense power whose future was unforeseeable. He could rise to any heights. He was not merely a newspaper-man but a financial wizard, a born publicist, a magnetic speaker, an astute politician and an uncanny judge of men. He could lift the top off one's head and look inside. Had he wished he could have been a multi-millionaire in the City of London, a Cabinet Minister at Westminster or a newspaper giant who could outshine North-cliffe. He was not content to be any one of these things alone. Within a few years he became all three.

Once he had made his mark as a Member of Parliament he decided to buy a newspaper. The *Daily Express* – owned by Sir Arthur Pearson who had gone blind, and edited by that brilliant and lovable man, Ralph D. Blumenfeld, an American Jew who had come to England and become more English than the English – was on the rocks. It was well-produced, well-written and edited by a man of genius. It lacked money. Blumenfeld, known to the whole of Fleet Street as R.D.B., went to the young Max Aitken, told him that he had difficulty in finding enough money to pay for paper and wages and asked him if he would loan the *Daily Express* some thousands of pounds. Aitken replied that he would do so willingly if the *Daily Express* would undertake to preach consistently his pet doctrine of Empire Free Trade. R.D.B. agreed. That was not only the beginning of Beaverbrook's eventual ownership of the paper but of the Empire Crusade which swept Britain like a patriotic prairie fire. It became a new faith and force in the political world. It shook the Tory Party to its foundations, terrified the Liberals and dumbfounded the Socialists. It has gone on doing so ever since.

A little later Max Aitken went to see Northcliffe. He told him that he thought of buying the *Daily Express*. He asked Northcliffe for his opinion.

'Don't,' Northcliffe advised. 'You'll lose your fortune. It'll be money right down the drain.' He snapped his mouth tight shut with that bulldog look which had frightened lesser men. Young Max Aitken regarded him quizzically with those cold grey eyes which could light with such sudden fire, and said with a dry smile, 'You're too late. I've got my hands on it already.' Northcliffe was not impressed – and showed it.

Within a few years the *Daily Express* was given a new lease of life. Not just a lease of life but a succession of eclectric shocks. It became the most hectic newspaper office in Britain. A hive of ceaseless energy. Beaverbrook had no time for the idle, the hidebound, the unimaginative or the disbeliever. For a few years he hired and fired with a speed and ruthlessness unknown in journalism before. Not even Northcliffe at the height of his dictatorship had sent so many journalistic heads rolling. Clearly I was taking a chance.

Behind this façade of intolerant ruthlessness the man who could not suffer fools gladly had a warm heart, a deep old-fashioned Christian faith and a rare gift of inspiring confidence, enthusiasm and friendship. You either adored him or hated him.

The one man who could handle him with cool calm understanding and a firm but gentle hand was R.D.B. He could tame the whirlwind. Beaverbrook had immense respect for Blumenfeld's knowledge of men and events. No London editor had a wider circle of influential friends than the one-time American Jew from Wisconsin. And he repected R.D.B.'s journalistic expertise. They made a remarkable and formidable combination. When I first met Beaverbrook, quite frankly I was terrified.

I had to go and see him in his top-floor flat at the old *Daily Express* offices in Shoe Lane. An old-fashioned, brick-built,

straight-faced Victorian building, its exterior grimy with generations of London smoke, inside there were wooden floors to all
the offices, a veritable fire-trap. The printing presses were deep
in the bowels of the earth. When they started up and began
churning out their nightly torrent of newspapers, the whole
building shook and clanked. The lift was archaic. Rats had free
run of the place. One could frequently hear them pattering along
the pipes.

Lord Beaverbrook constructed his own eyrie on the topmost
floor of this aged building. There he roosted like a watchful
eagle, keeping his brood of 'eaglets', as he christened his young
men, constantly on the prowl for news, the snapping-up of
scoops. His flat consisted of a sitting-room/dining-room, kitchen,
bathroom and a bedroom or two. He frequently slept 'on top of
the job'. This constant personal supervision, inspiration and
direct government spurred every man in the place. You never
knew when the boss would breathe down your neck.

When I first marched into the elm-panelled sitting-room to
meet the boss I felt, frankly, more apprehensive than I had done
on many a day in the trenches. There sat 'the little man', the
new Napoleon, at his desk with a battery of telephones in front
of him. He gave me a brief 'Good morning' and plunged into
business straight away. One dare not waste a word with him.
He had no time for untidy minds. I soon saw that I had to
watch my step carefully. Here was a man of needlelike per-
ception with no time for fools. He had an incessantly enquiring
mind. 'I want to know ... I must find out ...' These phrases
were the constant backbone of his conversation. He could turn a
man inside out and squeeze him like an orange until the pips
jumped.

I came out of that first interview feeling as though I had
plunged into a cold bath and come out with a glass of champagne
in my hand. Here was a man worth working for. He, in himself,
completely epitomized the *Daily Express* which he had bought
and revivified in his own mould. Together with the *Sunday Express* they were to be the double mirror of that active mind.

A week later the General Strike hit Britain a dangerous blow.
Trains, trams, buses and the Underground shut down. All the

printers went on strike. Shipping was paralysed. The stoppage was almost complete throughout the country. However, the telephone and postal services continued to function, and gas and electricity were not cut off.

Luckily the Government under Baldwin was well prepared. Volunteers from every class of the community moved in to maintain the essential services. They drove trains, buses and trams. They kept the London Underground moving, slowly but surely. The ordinary motorist almost without exception turned himself into a form of public transport. Thousands of special constables were sworn in. They included citizens from dukes to dustmen. A special Government newspaper, *The British Gazette*, was produced in the *Morning Post* building on the corner of the Strand and Drury Lane under the aegis of Winston Churchill. It was a newspaper of few pages, packed with official directions, news, views and facts.

Beaverbrook promptly decided to print his own newspaper even if it was a single news-sheet. The *Daily Express* must keep the flag flying. The superintendent of the *Express* printing works, the late – and great – S. W. H. Long, was loaned to *The British Gazette* as production manager. He was a typical John Bull working-class type who, by sheer energy and ability, had risen to become not only the top man in the printing organization of the *Daily Express* but to be appointed to the Board. He looked like the late Ernest Bevin, the Somerset farmer's boy who rose to be a Socialist Cabinet Minister and one of the best and most patriotic statesmen that Party has produced.

Sidney Long, who liked to demonstrate his working-class origin and sturdy working-class independence by marching into Beaverbrook's flat with his cloth cap on his head – which 'the little man' blandly ignored (thereby causing Long to drop the habit) – did a wonderful job. I am sure that if he were alive he would forgive me for reminding him of the story current when the General Strike ended: Sidney finally expected a knighthood since Churchill had said to him on the night when the strike ended: 'You've done a grand job. I shan't forget you.' Sidney, for the next few days, was reported to spend a long time looking at himself in the mirror, straightening his tie and murmuring confidentially: 'Sir Sidney – Sir Sidney.' Instead he was awarded a less sonorous honour.

My job during the strike was to find small printing-firms out in the suburbs with non-union staffs who would be willing to take the risk of printing our one-page newspaper. A sub-editor was allocated to each of these 'branch offices'. He got his flow of news over the telephone from the main office. He wrote his news-stories, had them set up in type, made up the page in proper form and had it run off the printing machine within an hour or so. The *Daily Express* paid the small printers heavily for the risks they took.

It was a real risk. Almost the first firm I approached was Fowler's of Cricklewood whom I had known since boyhood. Within a few days of printing the first news-sheet their works were besieged by a mob of thugs who battered down the doors and then smashed the type with hammers and put the works out of business.

I realised after the first day or so that there was leakage to the strikers concerning the whereabouts of my secret accomplices. I soon found that my motor-car was being followed by a motor-cyclist from the moment I left the *Daily Express* building. He was the spy who divulged the whereabouts of our 'branch offices'.

I foxed him by stopping en route at hotels and offices where I could go in at one door in one street and come out by another door in another street where another motor-car would be waiting to pick me up. The Piccadilly Hotel with its separate entrances in Piccadilly and Regent Street was a perfect example of this method of dodging the spy.

There was a dramatic interlude in the first week when a dray loaded high with gigantic rolls of newsprint (each roll represented five miles of paper) was being driven from the newsprint warehouse to the *Daily Express* office in Shoe Lane, a narrow alleyway off Fleet Street. It was drawn by two enormous shire horses, each weighing about a ton. These hairy-footed equine monsters came clattering down Ludgate Hill, into Ludgate Circus and were promptly surrounded by a mob of strikers who tried to bar their way. The strikers threatened the driver and his mate.

They argued fiercely with them. Two young *Express* reporters named Tom Darlow and Francis Williams watched this proceeding. The moment the driver and his mate, frightened by the strikers' threats, climbed down from the high driving-seat on the dray, Darlow and Williams dashed forward and sprang on to the dray. Darlow, who was a Norfolk farmer's boy and a giant in physique seized the driving whip and lashed the horses into a gallop. He drove straight at a bunch of strikers who tried to stop them. The strikers scattered like rabbits. Others tried to climb on to the back of the dray as it lumbered forward and turned the corner into St Bride's Street. Francis Williams who had a heavy club in his hand promptly banged heads and hands. Men fell off the dray like ninepins.

The whole equipage came charging up St Bride's Street at full gallop, the steel hooves of the horses striking sparks from the paved road. It was like watching a Roman war-chariot going into battle.

I was standing on the pavement with Lord Beaverbrook outside the St Bride's Street entrance to the offices. It was a moment of high drama – the horses charging up the street at the gallop, heavy wheels rumbling, Darlow shouting to his horses, strikers running after the dray and Francis Williams laying into them with his club. The huge clumsy equipage swung round the corner into the narrow alley of Shoe Lane, just wide enough to accommodate the dray.

A posse of police promptly cordoned off both ends of Shoe Lane and held the mobs at bay. The dray drew up at the unloading bay and a swarm of reporters, sub-editors, advertising salesmen and office workers unloaded the giant rolls which were hoisted off by a crane and lowered to the printing floor below street level. The strikers had been well and truly beaten.

Beaverbrook was so thrilled by that thunderous battle charge up St Bride's Street that he danced on the pavement with excitement and cheered on Darlow and Williams. When it was all over he sent for both young men.

'You have done a great job – an heroic job,' he said. 'Tell me what you would both like. I want to reward you.'

Instead of asking for a rise in salary, a fat cheque or a gold watch, both youngsters promptly said that they would like to be posted to the City Office where they could learn the mysteries of financial journalism. This was done.

Later Darlow became City Editor of the *Daily Herald* and Francis Williams was raised to the peerage as Lord Francis-Williams having made his mark as publicity adviser to Attlee, the Socialist Prime Minister of recent years. It was a sardonic quirk that both men, having been trained and praised by Lord Beaverbrook, the arch-apostle of capitalism, should end their days in the Socialist camp.

The strike collapsed a few days later. The attempt by organised Trade Unionism to hold the country to ransom failed utterly. The Law Lords dealt it the final shattering blow when they declared that it was illegal. What broke the strike perhaps more than anything else was the astonishing and utterly spontaneous reaction by the thousands of volunteers from all classes and of all ages who kept the wheels turning and the essential services in action. They were the true voice of Britain.

In the *Daily Express* office the whole complex telephone-system was operated by three women, Lady Louis Mountbatten, the Honourable Mrs Richard Norton and Mrs Freddie Doidge. On their shoulders fell the burden day and night of seeing that the news came in and was sent out. Beaverbrook praised them in one breath and gave them the rough edge of his tongue the next. They grinned and liked it. The twinkle in his eye took the sting out of the most acid backlash from his tongue.

Beaverbrook attracted outstanding characters as a magnet attracts steel. He surrounded himself, by a natural process of magnetism plus deliberate choice, with men of ability. The constellation of stars which revolved round the sun of Beaverbrook was dazzling. They varied in character background enormously. His right-hand man in business and finance was a tall, fresh-faced, quiet-spoken, undemonstrative Canadian Scot, E. J. Robertson. 'Robbie' was a serving soldier in France with the Canadian Army when Beaverbrook was the official 'Eye Witness' with the Canadian Armed Forces in the field. They were opposites in character and appearance but had a strong underlying affinity, particularly where money and business were concerned. 'Robbie' became the financial pilot of the *Daily Express* ship. His was the hand which curbed extravagance. His were the sharp eye and incisive mind which judged candidates for the staff before they were appointed. He was all steel on the outside but a man of infinite warmth and sterling friendship behind that slightly forbidding exterior. Integrity and probity were his middle names.

Another Canadian of a very different calibre was Beverly Baxter. He had been a piano salesman in, I think, Toronto, and hitched himself to the Beaverbrook wagon with a sharp opportunistic eye for the future. He played the piano with conscious flair and oozed conscious charm. He was bland, podgy, smooth and shallow. On his desk prominently displayed was a large signed photograph of himself inscribed in florid handwriting 'To Bax, That Prince of Good Fellows'. You were not allowed to miss it.

This piano-playing, light-opera songster who never failed on the slightest provocation to burst into the arias of *Madame Butterfly* was a slick, suave gossip writer. He could put pen to paper on almost any subject and you might be quite certain that if he could not probe or assay the depth of that subject he would at least give it in print a mirror-like surface in which was reflected the bland physiognomy of Beverly Baxter. If Beaverbrook was the medieval baron come to life, Baxter was his troubadour. He frisked around his master like a pampered poodle. Baxter was no fool. Equally he was no wise man. An opportunist of the first order who could turn his brittle talents to the shining advantage of the moment.

I doubt if he had a real friend. In this he differed markedly from R.D.B. who commanded the friendship and respect of high and low from Cabinet Ministers to office boys, or from 'Robbie' for whom every man of discernment had unshakeable respect and often a deep affection.

Baxter's dexterous opportunism reached its fine flower on that historic but hitherto unrecorded occasion when, at a later period, he became Editor of the *Daily Express*. Arthur Christiansen, a young journalist from Liverpool, son of a Mersey River passenger-boat skipper, had joined the *Daily Express*, made his mark and was tagged by Beaverbrook for rapid promotion.

He therefore sent Christiansen, Dick Plummer, another promising youngster (he later became Sir Leslie Plummer, Labour M.P. for Deptford and the architect of that disastrous waste of millions of public money, the infamous Ground Nuts Scheme), and one other young man up to the Manchester office for a gruelling apprenticeship among the hard men of the North with the promise that if and when the Northern edition of the *Daily Express* reached a million circulation they would all be brought back to London and given high office.

'Chris' did well. Beaverbrook resolved to make him Deputy Editor of the *Daily Express*. He rang up Baxter and said, 'Bax, I'm sending young Christiansen down from Manchester to be your deputy.'

'In that case, sir,' said Baxter suavely, 'I resign.'

'I am still sending Christiansen down to be your deputy.'

'Very well, sir, as I said, in that event I resign.'

'Whether you resign or not, Bax, I am still sending Christiansen down to be your deputy.'

To which Bax, out-flushed, replied lamely, 'In that case, sir, I withdraw my resignation.'

The editorial staffs of both papers glittered with men of ability. Hannen Swaffer, 'The Pope of Fleet Street', with his mane of white untidy hair, black silk cravat awry, his coat dusted with cigarette ash and his ascetic face lively with sardonic wit and satire, was perhaps the best-known theatrical critic of the day. J. B. Morton, the immortal 'Beachcomber', the erudite Oxonian disciple of G. K. Chesterton and Hilaire Belloc, contributed a column which was, and still is, unique – a blend of classical perfectionism with sharp satire and schoolboy jokes. On the few occasions when it has been left out of the paper swarms of readers' letters have testified to its extraordinary popularity. Then there was the other Morton, the great H.V. who, born an Armenian (like Michael Arlen the fashionable novelist of the day, who wrote *The Green Hat*), knew and portrayed the English and their countryside better than they know it themselves. George Strube, who was the best cartoonist of the era came, I believe, from Cambridgeshire farming stock, in spite of his odd surname. He was first recognised as a cartoonist of outstanding wit when customers noticed the clever little pen-and-ink sketches which decorated the bar of a pub in Well Walk, Hampstead, of which he was 'mine host'. Beaverbrook whipped him out of the pub and into a £10,000-a-year job.

Then there was that financial genius, S. W. Alexander, a dwarf of a man who bore a remarkable resemblance to Beaverbrook and on occasion would stand up to the great man with all the courage and fight of a cock-bantam. He made the City Pages of the *Daily Express*.

Before he reached this eminence he was Private Secretary to Beaverbrook. 'The little man' would sometimes glare at the even smaller replica of himself and demand, 'Naow tell me, Alexaander. Who was your faather? I know they all say that I am your faather. But *who* was he?' The problem, so far as I know, was never resolved. I personally never knew the answer to that question.

CHAPTER FIVE

The Gorgeous Lord Castlerosse

A Giant of Wit, Words, Wine, Women, Diamonds and Debts – The
Greatest Gossip Writer of This Era – The Fatal Doris – How We
'Trapped' Lord Riddell – The Deluge of Mrs Gamage – Castlerosse Is
Banned by Beaverbrook – Lloyd George Calls – And My Dog Insults
Beaverbrook – The Sad End of Castlerosse – 'A Lonely Lord with a
Hole in His Heart'

Into this curious dynamic world of bubbling energy and fierce
individualism there flared a new and brilliant comet. None less
than Valentine Edward Charles Browne, elder son of the fifth
Earl of Kenmare and a captain in the Irish Guards. He had
fought a good war, been wounded in the elbow and was now
determined to make the most of life. That is putting it in the
lowest possible key.

Valentine Castlerosse knew nothing of journalism and less of
business. He was a big man physically, and a far, far bigger man
as a spendthrift. Money flew through his fingers with the con-
summate ease with which epigrams flew from his tongue.

Physically he was enormous. He stood over six feet in his
socks, broad-chested as a barrel with a ruddy smiling moon of a
face, quick dancing eyes, a cat-like walk, high-pitched voice, and
a falsetto laugh which surprised one. You expected a masculine
bellow, like the trumpet of a bull elephant, to come out of that
enormous chest.

His mother was a Baring, one of that remarkable family of
merchant bankers who, as German Jews, came to this country a
century or so ago and in no time amassed a string of titles of
their own – Ashburton, Revelstoke, Cromer and so forth – as well
as marrying their way into the old aristocracy of the realm. The
present Earl Spencer is one of the brood. Castlerosse, through
his mother, was another. It would not be short of the mark to
say that there has never yet been a Baring who lacked financial
acumen, wit, oratory and a sharp eye for the main chance. They
have produced at least one outstanding statesman, that great
Proconsul of Empire, Lord Cromer.

The blend of Irish charm and warmth with the Baring quick-

54

wittedness and love of display made Castlerosse the notable character that he was. His Jewish blood probably accounted for the splendour of his dress which in any lesser man would have been branded as bad taste. He carried it off perfectly.

Everything he did was on a grand and gorgeous scale. Larger than life. Like Jamshyd 'he gloried and drank deep'. He was Lucullan in his food. And positively Bacchanalian in his drink. He was a gourmet but not a glutton.

He could write, as to the manner born, with infinite Irish charm and tenderness. Equally he could slash, thump and bludgeon with Johnsonian vigour. He could be infinitely courteous and sometimes unforgivably bawdy.

I met this astonishing man the day after I was appointed Advertisement Manager of the *Sunday Express*. Beaverbrook had dredged him up from the gilded morasses of the West End and given him the job of gossip writer. There has never been a gossip writer to equal him before or since. Although he had probably never written anything more dangerous than a cheque, he blossomed in the aura of Beaverbrook. His weekly page 'The Londoner's Log' was the most widely-read feature in journalism. Many people bought the paper first and foremost to read 'the Lord's Column'.

He burst on my vision the day after I was appointed Advertisement Manager. The door of my office opened and in strode this enormous man, rubicund, smiling, dressed impeccably in a black jacket and striped trousers, set off by a double-breasted white waistcoat which encased his vast chest and vaster stomach in a glow of virgin purity. That was the nearest he ever came to it. The whole effect was enhanced by a flashing diamond tiepin and diamond cufflinks. A prosperous bookie could not have done better. On Castlerosse it looked right.

'My name is Castlerosse,' said a high thin voice. 'Delighted to meet you. You must call me Valentine.' We chatted briefly. I took to him at once. I defy any man and certainly any woman to have failed to succumb to the Castlerosse charm.

His feminine victim – others said that he was *her* victim – at that time was the celebrated Doris Delevigne, a staggeringly beautiful Society girl whose good looks were matched only by the generosity of her favours. It was currently said that she had been kept by a syndicate of lovers, headed by a famous polo player, until the cynical man-of-the-world, Castlerosse, fell for her with the guileless ardour of an Irish boy. I knew the gossip and no more. I had heard also that Beaverbrook violently opposed the liaison and threatened to sack Castlerosse if he married her. He did so. It was fatal. Doris Delevigne killed his spirit and broke his heart. She was as hard as the diamonds she cost him.

To revert to those early days when Castlerosse was in his full glory. Beaverbrook might have regarded Baxter as his tinkling troubadour, but for years Castlerosse was his Falstaffian court jester. They got on splendidly. Castlerosse's page, witty, tender, outrageous, near-libellous, near-poetic, acid and inspired, pulled in the readers by tens of thousands. He was paid extravagantly. It was not enough. His appetite for luxury, regal living, food, wine, Doris, dress and cigars far outstripped the generous Beaverbrook payout. His debts snowballed to gigantic proportions. Beaverbrook paid them again and again. Robertson's puritanical straight-forward Scots mind writhed as the bills poured in.

'Raabertson,' Beaverbrook rasped one day, 'here's a new sackful of Valentines' bills. Who's going to pay them – you or me?' History does not recall.

I imagine that Valentine had comparatively little money to spend as a young man. His dear old father, a courtly, kindhearted, but relatively penniless Irish peer with thousands of barren acres of Kerry, had no great fortune in money. So when Castlerosse touched the fringe of the Beaverbrook millions, they went to his head. He lived and travelled like royalty.

His life was an Oriental extravaganza. His list of clubs alone was like a necklet of expensive gems – The Carlton, Guards', White's, St James's, Kildare Street (Dublin) and, of course, the Embassy Club in Bond Street and a string of nightclubs. The Savoy, the Ritz, Claridge's, and the Berkeley Hotels were his dinner platters. When he entered a restaurant, conversation stopped and all eyes turned on him. The head waiter invariably conducted him with a low bow and a discreet smile to the best table. Valentine sailed through life like a galleon, high-pooped and deep-waisted, superbly gunned with cigars. At one period when he was earning a great deal of money he rented a suite for months in Claridge's. Beaverbrook disapproved. Castlerosse disregarded him.

My colleague, James Wentworth Day, who was Chief Feature Writer of the *Sunday Express* at that time stayed with Valentine on the family estates in County Kerry and assures me that he (Castlerosse) was a superb rifle shot. Jimmy once saw him kill two galloping stags with a single shot. A feat which was described by the ghillie as 'His Lordship's gallery shot. He always does it to impress the veesitors.'

I can vouch for the fact that had it not been for the wounded elbow he certainly would have been a scratch player at golf. He might indeed have been one of the best amateur scratch players of the day. As it was, his wound, his bulk, and his temper which was sometimes uncontrollable and a little childish, reduced him to the state of a useful (and always entertaining) week-end golfer. I remember playing with him at Addington Palace Golf Course which he disliked intensely because it was hilly. He put up such a bad show that, in a sudden gust of temper, he snapped every one of his hickory clubs across his knee.

Since he and I both worked full time on Saturdays we had a full day off from the office on Monday. We usually went either to Addington or to Walton Heath which he much preferred. There, later on, he built himself a large bungalow, christened typically, 'RainbozeEnd', very lush and very plush. In those days there was no bungalow so we always took up a strategic position in the lounge of the clubhouse because we knew very well that, sooner or later, Lord Riddell, a great power in the *News of the World* organisation and chairman of George Newnes, the publishers, who incidentally owned *Country Life,* would heave in sight. George Riddell had started life as an office boy but he was a natural aristocrat with a clean, keen face, a clean, keen mind – which did not stop his fund of dirty stories – a rare sense of business honesty and a natural power to govern. No man deserved a peerage more richly. This was our victim.

We knew, as we sat expectantly on our settee, that the moment

His Lordship stalked in, like a greyhound, from the Dormy House where he lived, that he would greet us. This meant free drinks, free lunches and free green fees for both of us. If we nabbed him our day was made. If we missed him it was an expensive lunch. He was our permanent vein of gold. No one would have enjoyed the joke more than Riddell had we told him.

Came the day when the late Eric Gamage opened his great new store in Oxford Street almost opposite Selfridges. It was his challenge to Selfridge, then the store king of London. I naturally wanted to get big display pages of advertising from Gamage. What better method than to introduce to him 'the fabulous lord' – and make sure moreover that the latter wrote up the store in his page.

'Valentine' I said sternly, ' You dine too often off gold plate. You wallow in luxury like a divine swine.' He cocked a twinkling inquisitive eye and waited for the rest. 'It's time you learnt how we, the poor, live. It's time you came down to earth and ate with the ordinary folk, the people who read your column. Forget Claridge's for today and lunch with Eric Gamage in the public restaurant at their new big shop in Oxford Street. When they've lushed you up you can earn your keep by writing a nice piece about them for next Sunday. Is it on?'

'It is,' he squeaked and reached for his hat.

I had taken his acceptance for granted and had warned Eric Gamage to be ready to receive our bird of paradise. We arrived to find sherry and cocktails awaiting us in Eric Gamage's luxurious office. We were having our first glass of sherry when the door opened and in swept Mrs Eric Gamage in what was clearly her smartest day-dress. She affected complete surprise, apologized charmingly for coming in and said she had no idea that her husband was busy. I had quite another idea. Those smart clothes had not been put on for nothing.

'Would you very much mind, Lord Castlerosse, if my wife joins us for luncheon?' Eric asked.

'Good God, no.' Castlerosse squeaked. 'Such a lovely creature, so beautifully dressed, will take my mind completely off my luncheon. I shall therefore enjoy it all the more.' That clearly made the day for Mrs Gamage.

We were taken to a corner table commanding the great restaurant which was packed with people. The entrance of Castlerosse, gorgeously waistcoated, exuding supreme aristocratic self-confidence, caused all heads to turn. A twitter as of muted birds went through the great room. People nudged each other. There were whispers. The Grand Mogul of Fleet Street and the West End had deigned to shed the effulgence of his presence upon the ordinary man in the street and the ordinary woman with a shopping basket. The Gamage day was obviously made.

We sat down. The table was beautifully laid with silver, cut-glass, lovely china, and napery as spotless as Valentine's white waistcoat. I noticed beside the table a wine cabinet stocked with vintage hocks, rare clarets, champagne and burgundy. Obviously we were in for a 'do'. Valentine's eyes wandered not to the wine cabinet, but to a frieze of advertisement plaques round the walls which proclaimed 'Pilsener Lager on Draught.'

'What would you care to drink, Lord Castlerosse?' Eric Gamage asked solicitously, his mind obviously on Krug straight off the ice, or a cool, 1921 hock. It was a boiling hot day. Mrs Gamage rustled with silken expectancy. I guessed that she had set her sights on the Krug.

'Oh! – er,' said Valentine, switching his eyes from the wall advertisements. 'Drink, eh? Pint of lager, please. Just the stuff for a hot day like this. Draught Pilsener. Nothing to beat it.'

Mrs Gamage's face dropped a millimetre or two. Eric Gamage coughed suitably. 'Of course, Lord Castlerosse. I'm so glad you like the thought of our Pilsener. I'm going to have a pint of it myself.'

'So will I. Delicious,' cooed Mrs Gamage with a sweet smile banishing the Krug from her mind like a bad dream. I chipped in for a pint also. The beer was ordered.

A small boy-waiter with the face of an angel who had dropped straight from Heaven, clad in an immaculate white bum-freezer jacket, appeared silently bearing aloft on his right hand a tray containing four pint glass tankards of lager beer, foaming. It glittered like pale gold.

The boy's progress towards the table was soft and decorous – until he caught sight of Castlerosse. The vision of that enormous man, splendidly white-waistcoated, tucking his vast stomach half under the table, leaning back and chuckling like a sultan to his favourites, was too much for the child. He stared. He goggled. Here was Solomon in all his glory.

Very gently the tray, born aloft by his right hand, tilted. The boy was too paralysed with admiration to notice it. The next second he shot the lot into the expensive but unexpecting lap of Mrs Gamage. She was drenched from the waist down.

I regret to record that Castlerosse, the gallant, who had flattered the unfortunate lady so extravagantly burst into a roar of laughter. He slapped his knee, gurgled and shook with rolls of mirth. It was not chivalry at its best.

Mrs Gamage, to her credit, took the cue, and wetly giggled. Her husband looked grim. I tried to remember not only my face but the advertisements to come. Those lunching nearest us had a free 'Crazy Gang' bit of slap-stick.

Castlerosse, still quivering with mirth, leant across and said to his host, 'That's given me the best laugh I've had for a long time. Promise me, Eric, that you won't sack the boy.'

'Of course not,' said Eric. 'Don't be stupid. It was a pure accident.' And he shot the boy a glance loaded with daggers.

Soon after, the great Billy Butlin, the holiday camp king, opened another of his camps at Clacton on the Essex coat. There was to be a sumptuous inaugural luncheon. A special train plastered with Butlin posters was laid on from London to take the guests and bring them back again. Valentine and I travelled in state with the rest.

We were taken on a tour of the camp, organized with the usual Butlin thoroughness, and then ushered into a luncheon which would have done credit to a Roman emperor. There were two toastmasters in red jackets, not one. The Butlin touch.

When the luncheon was over Valentine decided that he was bored and wanted to get back to London. We made our excuses and caught an ordinary train back, not the Butlin Special. It was empty of passengers as we climbed into our first-class compartment. Then two men appeared, bustling along the platform. A score of empty carriages beckoned them. Instead they opened the door and stepped into our carriage where we had sprawled comfortably over the seats. We put down our feet and regarded them coldly. We both wondered why the devil they had got into our particular carriage. There must be something in the wind, I decided. Then one man produced a pack of cards. That clinched the matter. Card-sharpers! Sharks! We were the pigeons about to be plucked. I decided firmly that I would lose no feathers.

'What have you got those for?' the second man asked the man with the cards.

'Oh, I thought our friends here might care for a small game of poker – it's a dreary journey, so we may as well amuse ourselves,' the card-sharper replied. I decided not to be amused. Castlerosse, always ready for a flutter, agreed to play. At first I said I was not interested in playing. Castlerosse expostulated, 'Oh come off it, Bill. You've taken quids off me before' (Which was not true.) 'Now I might get my own back.'

'Well,' I asked, 'what are the stakes going to be? I'll play for pennies only. That's quite definite.'

The faces of the two strangers dropped. We started to play. Then the ticket collector arrived. Valentine and I fished out our first-class tickets. I watched the two strangers narrowly, deciding inwardly that either they had no tickets at all, or that they were travelling first on third-class tickets. One man produced a first-class ticket. The other, clearly the card-sharper, the man who had produced the cards, felt in his trouser pockets, pulled out a gold chain and displayed a small gold badge attached to the end of it. The ticket collector took one look at it, bowed almost double and murmured deferentially; 'I'm so sorry, sir, to have troubled you. If I can be of any service, sir, I am at your command.' He withdrew from the carriage backwards and bowed himself out.

'What sort of open sesame have you got on that chain, if I may ask?' I said to the card-sharper.

'Oh,' he said quietly, 'It's just a pass. I happen to be Chairman of this railway. We've been to Billy Butlin's luncheon and I got away early.'

After that I played for higher stakes. By the time we reached Liverpool Street I had lost fifteen pounds, so I promptly put in a bill for expenses at the office made out: 'To entertaining the

Chairman of the North Eastern Railway, £15.' The *Daily Express* paid up cheerfully. Valentine had the last laugh.

There was another occasion when I paid for Lord Beaverbrook and did not get my money back. He ordered Robbie, Castlerosse and me to dine with him at the Savoy Grill. It was early in the evening and his temper was sour. Something or someone had upset him. We sat down at our table and a chicken was produced. Chicken and green peas were his favourite foods. He prodded the chicken with a fork, decided it was too tough, picked it up and flung it across the room. Luckily it hit no diner. After that the meal proceeded with, shall we say, a certain atmosphere of restraint. At the end he announced briefly; 'Caam on! We're going to the pictures – the Empire in Leicester Square. We'll walk.' Castlerosses' face dropped a mile. He had dined well and had his bottle. The prospect of a long trek on hard pavement from the Strand to Leicester Square did not enchant him.

'The little man' got his hat and overcoat and set off at a brisk walk. He loved walking not only round his estate at Cherkley Court near Leatherhead, but also in London. Valentine would walk for miles over his Irish mountains but he hated hard pavements. In London he went everywhere in a taxi-cab or a Rolls. That night he lagged ponderously behind. When we arrived at the cinema, Beaverbrook, true to the royal image, said; 'I have no money. Needham, will you pay for the tickets?' I forked out two or three pounds and paid up. Valentine maintained a glum silence, I never saw the money back. After all, one could not very well put in an expense account to the *Daily Express*, itemized: 'To entertaining Lord Beaverbrook at the cinema, £3.'

Cherkley Court is a rather hideous mock-Gothic Victorian mansion of the sort that the brewers and city gents of the last century plastered all over the heaths, hills and wooded valleys of what was once rural Surrey. Beaverbrook loved the place, probably because of its far-reaching views. He walked for miles. He kept a small stud of hacks with a resident groom and rode many more miles on horseback.

Came the day when Castlerosse, having run up a string of extravagant bills – which Beaverbrook paid – was, not for the first time, sent to Coventry. He had been banned from the presence for weeks. Somewhere he was sulking in the shadows, but still dutifully turning out the gossip column that fascinated our readers.

Beaverbrook finally relented. He had a genuine affection for his prodigal son. He rang up Robbie with the usual preliminary peace formula since Robbie was the diplomatic mediator between the two when there had been a rift.

'Raabie, have you forgiven Caastlerosse? Shall we forgive him?'

'Well, sir,' said Robbie diplomatically, 'like the poor, he's always with us. '

'Well,' said 'the little man', slowly, 'I think I shall forgive him and invite him down to Cherkley. A ride on a horse will do his liver a lot of good. Pass the word to him.'

Valentine was delighted. He was to be received at the court of Cherkley once again. The lord and master had graciously unbent. The sun might now shine. The clouds had blown away. He was like a schoolboy going home for the 'hols'.

He went straight off to the most expensive saddler in the West End and ordered a brand new saddle. It had to be made specially to fit his gargantuan frame. 'And,' said he with magnificent finality, 'it must be delivered to me at Cherkley Court, Lord Beaverbrook's place in Surrey, not a moment later than nine o'clock next Sunday morning.'

He went down to Cherkley on Saturday in time for dinner. He was received if not with open arms at least with a tip-top meal and a bottle of champagne. The gates of paradise reopened. Next morning after an early and friendly breakfast the two men strode out to the front door exactly on time as the clatter of horses' hooves on the gravel announced that their steeds were ready. There stood their chargers, saddled and with a groom and a stable boy holding their heads. Castlerosse had but to put his foot into the stirrup and be eased into the saddle.

At that precise moment a Rolls-Royce swept round the corner and pulled up. A smart West End tradesman stepped out. He bore in his hands a brand new saddle and an envelope containing the bill. Beaverbrook, sensing the worst, snatched the envelope, ripped it open and read the bill. It made a hole in a hundred pounds. He rounded on Valentine like a tiger.

'Gaad dammit,' he rasped, transfixing the quivering Castlerosse with those cold grey eyes, 'you owe money to me and everyone else. Yet you perpetrate this extravagance. Aren't my saddles good enough for you? You will use my saddle and return this new one. If not, you never ride with me again.'

Back went the saddle to the dumbfounded tradesman. The Rolls swung round and bore man and saddle back to London. Castlerosse was heaved up by the groom into the Beaverbrook saddle and for the next hour rode in an Arctic silence.

One heard wild, but probably quite true, stories of monumental hotel and restaurant bills being sent to Beaverbrook, plus yard-long accounts for wine, cigars and particularly golf-clubs. Wherever Valentine played golf he invariably visited the professional's shop, went through the stock of clubs and ordered them by the dozen or half-dozen. When he died his effects included more than two hundred golf clubs, many of them unused and most or all, one may be sure, paid for by Beaverbrook.

Lloyd George had his country house and so-called 'farm' at Churt not far from Cherkley. There he played at farming on a hundred acres or so of almost pure sand, which were dosed endlessly with tons of fertilizer. This agricultural chemist-shop was used by him to give farming demonstrations to the Press at which the Welsh Wizard graciously allowed himself to be photographed striding behind the plough, clad in a dark city suit, a flowing black cape and a black felt wide-awake hat. 'Farmer Lloyd George' telling the farmers how to farm!

Lloyd George, who had sold more honours for cash that any Prime Minister in history, was a shrewd judge of the value of newspaper publicity. He was not a man to quarrel readily with his powerful neighbour at Cherkley Court. So one Sunday morning when the front-door bell rang, who should be standing on the door-step but the Welsh Wizard complete with black cape, long flowing white locks, drooping soup-catcher moustache, as sharp-eyed as a weasel. He had walked over to call on 'the little man'.

'Is the lord at home?' he asked the butler.

Driving myself in as Captain of Hendon Golf Club in the late twenties

The caddies race to retrieve the ball after I had driven myself in. The reward was a 'Jimmy o'Goblin' – a golden sovereign

Gordon Selfridge, the Colossus of modern stores advertising. The photograph was inscribed with the wise quotation: ' "To travel hopefully is better than to arrive. And all true success is labour." To L. W. Needham with best wishes'

Lord Beaverbrook. The photograph was inscribed 'Leslie Needham, from his friend, Beaverbrook'

'No sir, the lord is out walking.'

'Ah – on the water, doubtless.'

Cherkley was the scene of many business conferences between 'the little man', Robbie, Dick Plummer, Tom Blackburn, who was then General Manager of Beaverbrook Newspapers, and me.

At these conferences Beaverbrook, brought up in the evangelical atmosphere of his father's manse frequently addressed us in biblical parables and wrapped up his meaning in religious metaphors. He loved to weave a web of words as a change from the normal staccato machine-gun conversation on the telephone.

This was exemplified amusingly one day when four of us attended on him on the veranda overlooking the garden. We were Robertson, General Manager of the whole organization, with Dick Plummer as his assistant, Tom (now Sir Thomas) Blackburn, General Manager of the *Sunday Express*, with me as his assistant. Thus the four of us represented the affairs of the two main newspapers controlled by Beaverbrook.

We discussed first the affairs of the *Sunday Express*. Tom Blackburn, my immediate chief, made certain suggestions with which I disagreed. We had a friendly wrangle. Beaverbrook listened intently, commented briefly. When we had settled the affairs of the *Sunday Express* he turned his mind to those of the *Daily Express*. Instead of saying briefly to Blackburn and me, 'Thank you, you may now go,' he delivered himself of this priceless parable:

'Blackburn, you take Mr Needham down to the far caarner (corner) of the garden where you will find a row of beehives. They are full of bees. Pick up a twig, put it in the little hole you will find in front of the hive, stir it vigorously and all the bees will come out and sting Mr Needham. That's what you want, Blackburn, don't you?'

At that time I was living at Golders Green in a small house, very conscious of the fact that I had my foot on, shall we say, the second rung of the Beaverbrook ladder. A good job and naturally one wished to hold it. Therefore I studied the whims and electric reaction of 'the little man' with devoted care. He could override all opposition like a tank. The man who stood up to him was a brave man. None the less Beaverbrook respected

C

courage of that sort. And he could be quite astoundingly humble about his own shortcomings. This was one of his many lovable characteristics.

So we come to the Affair of the Dog. I owned a Great Dane. He had a bark like a train coming out of a tunnel. He was half as big as a pony. When I sat down to use the telephone at home he invariably laid his great head on my knee, sat on his haunches and listened in.

Beaverbrook rang up one morning before breakfast. I lifted the telephone. The dog laid his head on my knee. The familiar voice rasped, 'Needham I waant to tark to you. This is a serious matter. . . .' At that moment the front door bell rang. The dog let out an earth-shaking 'Woof Woof'. Beaverbrook's voice came sharply, 'Whaats' that, you say?' Another 'Woof'. I was desperate.

'Oh! shut up!' I admonished the dog. Beaverbrook heard. 'Whaat's that? See me at Stornoway House the moment you get to town. I shall expect you. This is serious.' He put down the phone.

This clearly meant the sack. You do not tell the Wonder of the Western World to 'shut up'. I missed my breakfast, and went by car on the wings of despair to Stornoway House, his mansion in Cleveland Row, St James's. I was shown into the library quaking inwardly. I had landed a good job and thought I was making progress. Now all was over. I braced myself as 'the little man' looked up from his desk.

'Good morning, sir,' I began. 'I do want to explain the circumstances about this morning's telephone conversation. . . .'

'Naow,' he brushed me aside. 'I know I'm bad on the telephone. . . .'

'But, sir, I must explain,' I blundered on.

'Not at aal. Don't explain. I know I'm bad on the telephone but Needham, you must realise that I have to use it a great deal in my business. Now I want to talk to you about So-and-So's advertising. That's what I rang up about.' He plunged straight into business and never learned that I had told my dog – not him – to 'shut up'.

On another occasion, trivial but amusing, I 'foxed' Lord

Beaverbrook on the telephone by using an assumed voice. Stanley Bell, Managing Director of the *Daily Mail* rang one evening to say, 'Bill, as one of my oldest friends, I want you to know that I have been fired. It'll be on the front page of the *Daily Mail* tomorrow morning. I'd rather you knew from me direct beforehand'. He was clearly upset and told me the full details.

'Come and stay at my house at Sunningdale,' I said. ' Hide yourself for a week or so. Let your mind settle down in peace. Give Fleet Street a miss for the time being.' He came gladly. His whereabouts were supposed to be a close secret.

Two nights later the telephone rang. I answered it. That familiar Canadian voice grated in my ear: 'I'd like to tark to Mr Stanley Bell. Is he there?'

'Who is speaking?' I asked in my fruitiest butler's voice. It seemed at the moment to be wiser if I, as one of his executive's, knew nothing of Mr Bell's whereabouts.

'This is Laard Beaverbrook.'

'Very good, my lord,' I said in a rich Jeeves tone of obsequiousness 'I will see if Mr Bell is available.'

I went to Stanley in the dining-room and whispered; 'The old man's on the phone. He wants you. Better not let him know you are here.'

It turned out that Beaverbrook who was dissatisfied with the general set-up of the Newspaper Proprietors' Association wanted the whole thing put on a more business-like footing with Stanley Bell as Managing Director. They had a long talk but nothing came of it. And 'the little man' never knew that Bell's butler was his own Bill Needham. Not long after I nearly did lose my job. Robertson was taken ill. I was told to step in as his deputy. I was then General Manager of the *Sunday Express* but became, for the time being, Deputy General Manager of the *Daily Express* as well. It meant a lot of responsibility and careful decision.

One day R.D.B., then Chairman and Editor-in-Chief, rang me and said that as the newly appointed Master of the newly-born Company of Newspaper Makers he was arranging a midnight matinée at the Royalty Theatre to raise funds for this newest City Company. He therefore instructed me to place a full-page advertisement for the *Daily Express* in the theatre programme for that night. I pointed out to him that it was against policy to place advertisements in any magazines which were published for charity. We were constantly approached by various charitable organizations and had a firm rule on the matter. Had we agreed to one we should have been overwhelmed by hundreds of other appeals. He brushed my objections aside.

'Nonsense, my dear Needham. I am the Chairman of the *Daily Express* and the Editor as well as being the first Master of this new City Company. So I have every reason to authorize you to go ahead with it.' He added, 'It's not a question spending the firm's money on the advertisement. I'll pay for it myself if you like.' I pointed out that it was a rigid principle and nothing to do with money. He insisted that the advertisement went in. So in it went.

The midnight matinée came. Who should turn up but Beaverbrook and Castlerosse. 'The little man' picked up his theatre programme, flicked over the pages, saw the full-page advertisement for the *Daily Express* – and exploded. Next morning I got the full blast on the telephone.

'Needham, what does this advertisement in the Royalty Theatre programme mean? You know full well that I forbid this sort of thing. It's a cast-iron principle. Why have you broken it?'

I explained that as R.D.B. was personally involved and had argued and pleaded with me I had reluctantly agreed to the advertisement, more especially as he had insisted upon his right to give me the instruction as an order.

He listened and then said, 'Now I'll tell you what I want you to do, Needham. You will sit down and write me a letter of resignation. Don't worry – I shall not accept it. But I want your resignation in writing. Then I shall explain to R.D.B. that he has cost me the resignation of Mr Needham, one of my up-and-coming young men. Write that letter now.'

The future was bleak. After all, he might accept the resignation. I went to R.D.B. in a devil of a quandary and explained things. He listened sympathetically but protested that he and Beaverbrook were on equal terms and that it was ridiculous for

Beaverbrook to demand my resignation simply because I had obeyed his (R.D.B.'s) order.

In the middle of the conversation R.D.B.'s secretary came in and said that Lord Beaverbrook was on the telephone for Mr Needham. Would I take it in R.D.B.'s office or would I go back to my own. I thought it more tactful to take it in my own office. I rushed down the corridor, lifted the phone and the voice came through: 'Needham, don't write that letter. Good-bye to you.' He rang off.

Clearly he had decided that the incident did not warrant a head-on collision with R.D.B., the one man in the organization capable of standing up to him. Beaverbrook would probably have welcomed the chance to humble R.D.B. on a major issue, but the enforced resignation of young Needham was not a major issue.

The truth was that although Beaverbrook admired that wonderful old man R.D.B. and recognised his supreme mastership of the craft of journalism and the wider spheres of editorial know-how, he could not, in his own restless mind, reconcile this with his own drive for supreme power. Nonetheless the men remained firm friends for life.

When R.D.B. died, Beaverbrook told his widow, 'You have my deepest sympathy. He was a great and a wise man. I mourn him as a friend just as you mourn him as a husband. You have nothing to worry about, my dear, so far as the future is concerned. I will see that his salary is paid to you for the rest of your life.' And it was. 'The little man' may not have realized that Mrs Blumenfeld was a singularly hearty old lady. She went on enjoying life – and R.D.B.'s salary – till the age of ninety-three or thereabouts.

Meanwhile the Beaverbrook/Castlerosse partnership was creaking under the strain of irresponsible debts. Valentine's reign as court jester was on the wane. His marriage with Doris had broken up. Later she, poor thing, committed suicide. Her season as the highly expensive Society butterfly also came to an end.

The Castlerosse reputation in the public eye was of course high. He was still an impressive figure. One of the film companies approached with a glittering offer. Valentine rose to it like a trout at a fly. He left the Beaverbrook pool and landed in the waters of film-stardom with a splash. Meanwhile he married again. His bride was Thelma, Viscountess Furness, a hard-faced fashion plate. She was a daughter of the late Harry Hayes Morgan, the American Consul-General at Buenos Aires. She came to England as one of a small covey of coronet-hunting American good-lookers. In no time she was a prominent ornament of the café society of the day and a close friend of the Prince of Wales, later Edward VIII. She married Lord Furness a newly-minted Viscount of the rich shipping family. He also had a fortune in iron, steel and coal. Thelma set her sights high. She had already been married and she divorced Furness in 1933. I never knew whether she caught Castlerosse or Castlerosse caught her. Those two glittering fish swam in the same expensive stream. He may well have been after her money, equally, she would adore becoming a countess since Valentine had then succeeded his father and was Earl of Kenmare.

A year or two after he had left the *Express* he wandered into my office without warning, planted his great backside on my desk and said expansively, 'Bill, you old b——. You can take me out for a drink. I haven't seen you for a long time. A bottle of champagne will do us both good.'

I protested that it was too early in the evening to start drinking and that I had work to finish. 'To hell with that!' was the answer. And he practically swept me out of the office.

I took him to the American Club in Piccadilly and there we had a drink or two. Other members persuaded him to make a fourth at bridge. One of the players was that lovable little man the late Rt. Hon. J. H. Thomas, one of the most popular Cabinet Ministers that the Labour Party ever produced. Jim Thomas had started life as a railway man and had dropped his aitches as resoundingly as he had shovelled coal. He was a wonderful raconteur, beloved by Tories and Socialists alike. Castlerosse, therefore, was in his element, especially as he saw a chance of picking up a few pounds at the game. The evening drew on. The game finished. He rose to his feet a few pounds richer and with an expansive smile said, 'Come on, Bill. Back to my flat in Grosvenor Square; we'll have a drink there.' I was anxious to see the new set-up and went.

The butler opened the door, gave me a sour look and grudgingly let us in. I have never seen a man display such deliberate ill-manners.

We went into the dining-room and Valentine said to the man, 'Bring in some whisky, and tell her ladyship that I am here with a friend.'

The butler stared at him with dumb insolence, produced the whisky grudgingly and went off to acquaint the fabulous Thelma of our arrival. A moment later she swept in like an icy blast. She was tall, commanding, sharp-featured and sharp-eyed. She regarded me with Arctic distaste. I had been at their wedding, at Brompton Oratory, as an honoured guest but was now quite clearly an unwelcome past.

'You know my friend Bill Needham,' Valentine said.

She looked at me icily and said 'I must tell you, Mr Needham that you are not a welcome guest. No friend of my husband is welcome. He has gone through all my money and, worse than that, drunk my cellar dry. He told me that he was earning a fabulous salary with the film company and that he had a large share-holding in the Guinness organization.' I smiled inwardly knowing that he had mortgaged his Guinness shares, lost his income from Beaverbrook and that the film company was not too enthusiastic. She went on, 'He's got no money. And I must tell you that his friends are not welcome here. Good evening.'

The end was not far off financially and physically for that attractive, lovable and misguided friend. What I noticed particularly at this time was the marked manner in which Castlerosse and Beaverbrook missed each other. Valentine was in a state of almost continuous dejection. His gay, volatile, amusing personality had wilted. He was like a sunflower which no longer caught the sun and was drooping to seed.

Beaverbrook showed also that he missed the stimulating company of his court jester. Valentine had infuriated him times without number but he had made him laugh many more times than he had caused him to frown. I think that both men would have given a great deal to have made it up again and to re-capture the old joyous spirit. The rift had gone too far. We in the offices of the *Daily* and *Sunday Express* also missed the stimulus of Castlerosse's wit, the electric atmosphere between the two men. Something tangible, yet intangible had gone out of the lives of us all.

Not long after, the Kenmare estate lawyers told him bluntly that he must cut adrift from London and all his expensive West End tastes and habits, and retire to the solitude of his house at Killarney. It was a converted stable block of the original Kenmare House which had been burned down by the Irish rebels during The Troubles. A fair-sized house of great comfort with breath-taking views up the lakes of Killarney to the Gap of Dunloe with the ruins of the original Castle Rosse, from which he took his courtesy title, standing at the head of the lake.

There, to his tenants and cottage people, he was still 'the lord'. A lonely lord with a hole in his heart. He was alone with his mountains, his red deer on the skyline, his fallow deer and Japanese deer in the deep birchen wood. Trout in the lakes and a golf course on the shores which was inspired by Castlerosse himself and laid out by Henry Longhurst. Here Valentine showed the true touch of his own artistry. He decreed – that is the proper word – that each hole should be embellished by flowering shrubs. Thus one found the Lilac Hole, the Azalea Hole, the Laburnum Hole, the Rhododendron Hole, the Broom Hole and so on.

A life amid such peace and beauty would have been more than enough for most normal men. Valentine could enjoy it for brief wholehearted spells, but he was too gregarious a soul not to miss the glamour of the newspaper world, its stress and clamour and the cheerful fellowship of his London clubs. He pined inwardly. His health grew worse. He was a very sick man.

One day a large motor-car drew up at the front of his stables-home. Out got an old friend, the Managing Director of the Gillette Razor Company and his wife. Valentine was pathetically delighted to see them. He made them stay not only for drinks but for dinner and begged them to remain for the night. They told him that, alas, they were staying in Cork and must get back there.

'Then you must come and see me in the morning,' he insisted. 'I shall look forward to it. You've done me a lot of good.' he waved them farewell. Next morning he lay dead.

CHAPTER SIX

Beaverbrook in Tears

His 'Simple Faith in God' – The Tragic Playboy – The Incredible Strube – From a Pub To £10,000 a year – Swaffer, 'The Pope of Fleet Street' – Arnold Bennett 'An Overblown Duke' – His £20,000 a year – 'One Year to Live' – Tom Innes, the Buccaneer Editor – How to Make a Comic Writer – John Gordon, the Great De-Bunker – Is he a Millionaire?

I do not know how the death of Castlerosse affected Beaverbrook emotionally. Knowing them both so well I would say that the death of his court jester moved 'the little man' profoundly. There had been a long love-irritant relationship. The two utterly opposing personalities suited each other, in diverse way, as to the manner born. Each was the perfect foil to the other's particular brand of genius. One can well imagine, therefore, that Valentine's death reduced 'the little man' to secret tears.

Those who do not know Beaverbrook closely may scoff at the idea of anything reducing him to tears. The outside world, particularly the cynics of Fleet Street, saw only the image of the hard-driving go-getter, the ruthless Canadian, the man who proclaimed publicly that all men were 'too old at forty,' the man who engaged his editorial staff on a fortnight's trial and fired them instantly if they failed to make the grade – these critics could not imagine that 'the little man' would weep genuine tears of sorrow. I have seen him do so.

When his first wife, that delightful, feminine and appealing woman Gladys, a daughter of the Canadian General Drury C.B., died in 1927 I sat behind him at the funeral service. He was between his two sons, Max and Peter, with his head bowed, his shoulders shaking as he sobbed. The truth was that Beaverbrook had the emotional qualities which one would expect from his Presbyterian-Scottish upbringing in the backwoods of Canada. He was a man of the earth, with a simple faith in God and in the better sides of human nature. When he cried it was not for effect but a spontaneous expression of real sorrow.

I saw this again at the funeral service of that brilliant cartoonist George Strube, the ex-publican from Hampstead who became one of the most highly paid men in Fleet Street, well into the five-figure standard. 'The little man 'had a real affection for many of his staff. They were not only his workers, but his friends. When Strube died there was a memorial service at a Fleet Street church. Beaverbrook sat, stony-faced, through the service. When it was all over and we were filing out, Mrs Strube went up to him and thanked him for attending the service. He shook hands with her without a word. Then I saw the stony face break. His lips twitched. Tears started to his eyes and ran down his cheeks. He turned his head away like an embarrassed youth.

I saw a similar and more harrowing example of his deep emotionalism when the body of his younger son, Peter, who had died in Scandinavia in a sailing accident was brought back to England and lay in the library at Cherkley Court before burial.

E. J. Robertson and I went down from Fleet Street to offer our sincerest sympathy and that of the staff to Beaverbrook. He received us, white-faced, taut and gruff. He was obviously trying to hide his emotion.

'The boy's body is in the library if you want to see him,' he said almost brusquely. Robertson went in to view Peter who had been the playboy of the family, the dashing racing-motorist, the adventurous sailor, a bright light of the West End. Peter was at the time of his death attached to me for training as it had been decided that his playboy days had better end and that he should learn to take a serious part in the running of his father's empire. Beaverbrook stood silent beside me whilst Robertson went in to pay his last farewell to the boy.

When he came out 'the little man' turned to us both and said, 'Let us hope that he has gone to a happier life than he knew here. '

Then, suddenly, the barrier of restraint broke down. His face twitched and tears flooded his eyes. For a moment he was an old, broken man, a stricken father. Then he brushed the tears away, turned to us both and barked, 'How's the paper doing?' He plunged into business question-and-answer without stopping. That was his armour-plate against the sudden show of deep emotion.

I must go back to that lovable and singular little genius, George Strube. He was short and tubby, with a slightly olive skin, quick bright eyes, a slow deliberate manner which belied his electric mind, and he called everyone, including his wife, 'George'.

I do not know his origin but I believe he came of farming stock in the Cambridgeshire Fens. That could account for his foreign name, since many Dutch and Flemish drainers settled in the Fen Country from the time of the Stuarts onwards. Strube may then well have been of Flemish or Belgian descent.

He was, I believe, first discovered by a member of the editorial staff who used to frequent the pub in Flask Walk, Hampstead of which Strube was landlord. There George drew cartoons of his regulars to amuse them. It was clear that the man had a natural genius for character drawing. Presumably this was reported to R.D.B. The result was that Strube was invited to contribute to the *Daily Express*. At first he drew his cartoons at home, brought them to the office by taxi-cab, had lunch in Fleet Street and then returned to Hampstead, to Flask Walk, to clear up the bar after the midday customers had gone and prepare for the evening rush. Eventually he was given a full-time office at the *Express* and a salary of round about £10,000 a year. It was he who created that lovable little character, 'John Citizen', short, tubby, bespectacled, with a scrubby, drooping moustache, a bowler hat, an umbrella and an unquenchable spirit who, in some respects, was not unlike Strube himself. One could describe 'John Citizen' as the middle-class civilian equivalent of Bruce Bairnsfather's immortal war-time soldier 'Old Bill'.

I was fascinated to watch Strube at work. He had none of the immediate economy of line and instant inspiration of, say, Phil May or David Low, both of whom could express a person or a characteristic in a flash and with a minimum of line. Strube, on the other hand, had a series of mirrors fitted up in his studio. Thus, if he wanted to draw his 'victim' with an upraised arm, he would raise his own left arm so that it was reflected in one or more mirrors. Then, with one eye on the mirror and one on the drawing pad, he drew the arm in a few swift incisive strokes.

This is no derogation of his ability as a draftsman or cartoonist. After all, George Stubbs, the greatest English animal-
painter whose pictures of horses command tens of thousands
today, had a dead horse hung up in his studio so that he might
get every muscle accurate. He crowned that by hanging up a
dead tiger which he had procured from a zoo in Piccadilly. I
never, however, saw George Strube hang up a dead politician.

The *Express* in those days was a beehive of natural 'characters'. Beaverbrook attracted them like a magnet. Eccentrics of
all sorts, provided they had genius and the ability to express it,
had their niche on the paper. The most flamboyant of all was the
famous Hannen Swaffer, 'the Pope of Fleet Street'. There has
only been one Swaffer. There will never be another. He was a
first-class journalist, the best-known theatrical critic of his day,
possibly the greatest egoist of all time, a man whom you could
describe as mountebank, exhibitionist and unbearable extrovert.
He could be rude in word and print. The personal pronoun took
up most of his prose. Northcliffe, for whom he worked for a
good many years, always called him 'Poet'. I do not think Swaffer
ever wrote a line of poetry in his life, or was capable of doing
so. He edited *The People* for that curious Canadian financial
acrobat known as Colonel Grant Morden, when *The People* was
in a bad way. 'Swaff', demanded a top salary and ten per cent of
the profits, if any. He put *The People* on its feet.

He also edited the *Weekly Dispatch* – later known as the
Sunday Dispatch – for Northcliffe, who gave him his first job
on the *Daily Mail* in 1902 when Swaffer was 24 years of age.
During a long life as reporter, dramatic critic, gossip writer
and editor he served on the *Daily Mail*, *Weekly Dispatch*, *Daily
Mirror*, *Daily Sketch*, *Daily Graphic*, *Sunday Times*, *Daily Express* and, finally, the *Daily Herald*. Few working journalists
knew more about the inside workings of the popular daily newspapers than this extraordinary character.

Swaffer was tall, thin, pale with the long, ascetic face clean-
shaven, of an old actor, with flowing, uncombed grey locks on
which perched a broad-brimmed black trilby hat of the sort
affected by the old-time actor. He wore no collar or tie but
swathed his neck in a voluminous black silk cravat tied in a sort

of bow after the style of the Parisian Left Bank artists of the day. The general effect was enhanced by a long black flowing cloak, a short black jacket, black waistcoat and black trousers. The whole façade was streaked and powdered with cigarette ash. Add a pair of long delicate hands and you have the picture of one who stepped straight out of the pages of *Trilby*.

This affectation of Bohemianism hid a remarkably acute, incisive mind. He loved the theatre and knew the stage and stage-people inside out. He was equally a first-class news-getter. He could write an informed provocative and sometimes scandalous gossip column just as easily as he could write a leader or edit the whole paper. He had friends, acquaintances or enemies in every stratum of society, politics and finance.

In the Northcliffe era he drank heavily. Each day he held court at luncheon and often after the theatre in the Savoy Grill. Swaffer's table attracted notabilities and publicity-seekers like bees to honey. In those days he was seldom completely sober.

Northcliffe knew only too well that the abnormal stress and strain of daily journalism, where every minute is a race against the clock, leads men to drink. His patience, however, cracked one day when, coming down the staircase of the *Daily Mail* from his sacrosanct Room One he encountered Swaffer staggering up the stairs lurching from one side to the other. He stopped him and said, 'Swaffer! There's far too much drinking going on in this office. I am very concerned about it.' He looked at 'The Poet' accusingly. Northcliffe could be frightening.

'I-I-I know, chief,' Swaffer stuttered. He always stuttered, drunk or sober. 'You're d-d-dead right, chief. W-w-w-wait till I get to the top of these d-d-damned stairs and I-I-I'll f-f-f-fire some of the b-b-b——s!'

Northcliffe who had a tender spot for his 'Poet', shook his head resignedly and went on downstairs. No one was fired.

Whatever the story might be, Swaff had to be the centrepiece. He murdered modesty at its birth. He did it openly and without excuse. 'The d-d-difference between y-y-you and m-m-me,' he would say to a young bumptious journalist, just down from Oxford, 'is that *I know*.'

He reached the peak of self-praise when describing a royal

procession along the Mall, which he had been sent to report. He described the scene, as he saw it from the front row of the crowd lining the route, in these words:

'Th-th-they were all there. The K-k-king and Queen in an open c-c-carriage, the D-d-duke of Connaught on a horse, the d-d-damned Kaiser looking as uppish as usual and h-h-half a hundred other royalties with the c-c-cavalry clattering along in f-f-front and behind them. The crowd was cheering like m-m-mad. Just as the royal c-c-carriage got abreast of m-m-me, the K-king jogged the Qu-queen in the ribs, pointed at m-m-me and said out loud; "G-good G-god, Mary! There's old S-swaff!" '

Swaffer who boasted proudly that he came of Kentish yeoman stock – although his enemies swore that he was of German descent – could none the less laugh at himself. That was his saving grace. Moreover he did much kindness by stealth. He helped many a struggling actor and young actress either with a printed pat on the back in his theatre columns or with an introduction to the right producer at the right moment. The top right-hand breast-pocket of his ash-spattered jacket was usually stuffed with banknotes. If he ran across a reporter who was out of a job or a poor third-rate little actor who was 'resting', Swaff would, if he liked the man, stop him with a prod in the waistcoat button, fish out a fiver from his breast-pocket, press it into the man's hand and sweep on muttering, 'D-d-don't damn well thank m-me. Forget it.'

His reign at the Savoy Grill ended when one night a pretty and comparatively young actress, I think an American, whose performance he had slated unmercifully in his column, got up from a nearby table, walked across to him and said; You've been asking for this for a long time.' And smacked his face resoundingly. He never went back. Thereafter he held court in the Ivy Restaurant and elsewhere.

Swaff got on well with Beaverbrook of whom he wrote: 'I can only speak of the man I know – a kindly and helpful friend.' He went on to say in one of his own books, *Hannen Swaffer's Who's Who* (of which I treasure his signed copy: 'Wishing Bill Needham all that his fine character deserves') these words:

'When, before I joined him [Beaverbrook], I was present at one of his conferences, waiting until he could see me about some private matter, I heard him discuss, for nearly an hour with his managers, the details of some trifling difficulty with one of the mechanical unions. It seemed very stupid to me, and very wearisome.

'Northcliffe would have said "Yes" or "No" in a minute – and then, perhaps, been wrong. Beaverbrook listened to every word from everyone, except that, with the irritating way he has of asking questions, he would cross-examine and keep on asking more.

' "Your patience is astonishing," I said, when the others had gone. "I could not put up with a dreary argument over a petty thing like that."

' "I want to know all about it," he replied. "I am learning journalism now."

'Then he plunged into my troubles, and with a most helpful and considerate kindness.

'One of Beaverbrook's editors met me once when he had just had two hours of cross-examination.

' "It sounded as if the old man was trying to trap me," he said. "I had to be careful because I know he will start asking the same questions again, next time I see him, and I shall forget to give the same answers." '

Swaffer should be remembered for all time in daily journalism as the inventor of the daily gossip column. One might say that he also invented the theatrical writers' column.

That great journalist, novelist, thriller writer, playwright and Fleet Street all-rounder, the late Edgar Wallace, who was no respecter of persons and always spoke his blunt mind once wrote: 'There is only one man in the world who understands Hannen Swaffer – and that is I.

'Swaffer himself does not understand much about him. He accepts himself as one of the gifts of God, just as he accepts sunlight and spring flowers, and other lesser creations of the Almighty. The world revolves about him once in every twenty-four hours; for his special benefit the year is divided into four quarter-days. These are facts that are hardly worth analysing;

why he should be so gifted, *why* any revue is not complete without a reference to him and no musical comedian, whether he is appearing in London or Manchester, can resist a jape at his expense or an appreciation of his acknowledged qualities he does not trouble to discover.'

Today Swaffer is virtually unknown in Fleet Street except to the old hands. The new young journalists with their slick gossip-writers' approach to things have never heard of the man who invented gossip writing. The pompous, long-winded, dramatic critics of the heavier Sunday journals who delight in using words of six syllables where two would do, gaze down their fleshy noses with scorn at the dramatic critic of the twenties and thirties who could make or break a career or a production overnight. Swaffer could be vulgar, egotistical, satirical or rude but he was never boring. Most of the respectable Sunday critics of today were apparently born to bore.

In those days Swaff was so popular and so copied that a dramatic critic on a North-Country newspaper unashamedly labelled himself 'The Swaffer of the North'. Immediately the critic of a well-known West-Country newspaper had printed on his visiting cards the blistering statement that he was 'The Hannen Swaffer of the West.'

Would that we had a Swaffer today. Then the self-opinionated young men of Fleet Street would have a master to follow and a model to copy.

Beaverbrook had the knack of hooking the best men of the day to write to his popular papers. When Arnold Bennett was in the net we had something to talk about, something to advertise on the posters. Bennett, who had a quiff like a cockatoo, looked like an untidy butler and had a squeaky voice which grated on the ear, was probably the most successful playwright, author and journalist of the decade. He loved 'high life', expensive restaurants, good wine and Lucullan meals. He came from the lower-middle class, but he lived like a rather overblown and somewhat vulgar duke. His literary criticisms in the *Evening Standard* were at that time the best that Fleet Street has known for many years. And he had the rare distinction of having a wife who actually exposed their married life in an article in a daily newspaper, in which she said: 'It is hard to get on with a genius.' One day she asked Swaff 'Why do I only get sixpence a word for my article? My husband gets three shillings a word.'

'If you were not Mrs Arnold Bennett,' Swaffer replied, 'you wouldn't get anything.' That set her back on her haunches.

Swaff was a great admirer of Bennett's books but he had no time for Bennett's articles. Swaff wrote at the time:

' "The Old Wives' Tale" after Dickens, is, perhaps, England's finest record of ordinary people's lives. It is a work of genius. I cannot imagine its author writing, as he does, such drivelling journalism – "How to Get Thin", and that sort of thing – at £100 a time. Still, the rich must live, I suppose.

'With the exception of his literary articles and the one called "My Religion" I have never yet succeeded in reading one of Arnold Bennett's articles all through.'

We paid Bennett £300 per article, a very high rate indeed, and nothing to be sneered at in these days of inflation. I have heard it said that he was earning £20,000 a year in those days from plays, books and journalism.

The *Sunday Express* at that time had an odd editorial arrangement. The Editor-in-Chief was James Douglas, a gentle, mild-mannered Scot with a lined and ruddy, clean-shaven face, white hair and a quizzical eye. He must have had a singularly fortunate contract because he seldom came to the office but seemed to spend most of his working time at home in a tall Victorian semi-detached house with a pillared portico away in the genteel wilds of Bayswater. There the gentle Douglas meditated philosophically upon the current sins of mankind – and womankind – and wrote didactically and blisteringly upon them each Sunday. When Jimmy Douglas trumpeted, the world of London shook.

I remember one particularly earth-shattering cri de coeur which shouted from the placards: CONSTIPATION – THE ROOT OF ALL EVIL.

When that now-forgotten book *The Well of Loneliness* which laid bare the soul of Lesbianism (if it has a soul), to a public which hitherto had hushed up the fact, Douglas went to town in a big way with a headline an inch high which proclaimed: A book that must be burned. The result, of course, was that the book, which otherwise might have had a moderate sale, rocketed. New editions came hot from the press. Sales reached a staggering total. I remember seeing the authoress turn up at one first night after another self-consciously arrayed in what looked like a German officer's military field coat in the authentic field grey, with high collar, and near-regimental buttons. She had a pale face and a highly superior air. I forget her name.

Perhaps Jimmy Douglas's most dramatic effort to better the lot of mankind was his attempt to discover a certain diagnosis of, and cure for, cancer. It began when an old Fleet Street journalist suffering from cancer had been given by his doctor one year to live. So the old man, a true journalist to the last, appealed to Beaverbrook to allow him to write a leader-page article entitled 'One Year to Live' in which he would expound the philosophy of a man under sentence of death. The offer was accepted. It was bound to be a best-seller.

At about the same time a certain little Dutch doctor announced that he had perfected a method of diagnosing cancer faultlessly, through blood tests. At that time many suspected victims of cancer were operated on upon a more or less hit-or-miss method. No one really knew what was wrong with them until they were opened up. Obviously a sure method of diagnosis would be a Godsend. The Dutch doctor announced at the same time that he had perfected an almost sure cure for cancer.

Jimmy Douglas at once sought the backing of the top men in the medical profession. He promised the Dutch doctor the fullest publicity. Then armed with a set of test tubes which contained blood specimens from known cancer patients as well as blood taken from normal healthy people, he went over to Holland and asked the doctor to pronounce his verdict upon the various specimens, none of whose origins were indicated. The result was that the Dutch doctor identified the cancer blood specimens perfectly. This was tremendously exciting. Meanwhile the article 'One Year to Live' had been published on the leader page of the *Sunday Express*. It aroused tremendous national interest.

The *Sunday Express* capitalized it by announcing that the old journalist was to be sent to the Dutch doctor's clinic for treatment. The result was awaited by thousands of readers with bated breath. Shortly the old journalist despatched another article from Holland in which he announced that having undergone the preliminary stages of treatment he felt much better. Would he survive? Had the cure for cancer been found at last? Was this the discovery that would save perhaps millions of lives in the future? These were the questions which the man in the street asked.

Meanwhile I had given a dinner party in a private room at the Savoy to a number of eminent surgeons, all specializing in cancer, to meet the Dutch doctor. James Douglas as Editor-in-Chief and Tom Innes, the Managing Editor, were among the highly important guests. I remember to this day the earnest eagerness with which those distinguished surgeons listened to the Dutchman's exposition. He was questioned minutely. His answers seemed to satisfy everyone. The universal verdict was that if he could produce a certain method of diagnosing cancer faultlessly it would be of immense benefit to surgery and to humanity. Never, perhaps, had the tide of hope in medicine run higher. At the end of the dinner one or two of the leading surgeons in London asked the Dutch doctor if he would divulge his secrets. They pointed out that unless he did so, whatever his discovery might be, it would be of no benefit to surgery as a profession or to humanity as a whole. To our utter amazement he refused flatly to divulge anything.

'It is my secret,' he announced. 'I keep my secret. I shall make much money from it.' And not another word could we get out of him. The evening founded on such high hopes ended with a dull flop.

A day or so later I asked the little Dutchman to have lunch with me alone in the Savoy Grill. We sat at a table for two surrounded by a chattering fashionable throng. Actors and actresses, playwrights and authors, business men and advertising tycoons, rich Americans and Midland manufacturers, all busy with their own business, talking their heads off, surrounded us.

I begged the little Dutchman, in subdued tones, to think better of his blank refusal to communicate his secrets before he left for Holland. He must have had a conscience, for he sprang suddenly to his feet, flung out his arms, and at the top of his voice delivered an impassioned speech in which he thanked me for the lunch, the *Sunday Express* for its support and James Douglas for his interest, adding, with a final high-pitched flourish that his secret could save thousands of lives – but that he was keeping it to himself. The entire Savoy Grill stopped talking and eating for at least two minutes.

Shortly afterwards came the shattering news that the old journalist, whose article predicting recovery had cheered thousands of cancer sufferers, had himself died. Thus ended our great cancer campaign. Never did high hopes collapse more catastrophically.

Tommy Innes, then Managing Editor, was a superb 'character' in his own right. He should have been a buccaneer under Drake or Frobisher, in the golden reign of Queen Elizabeth the First. He was born to singe not only the beard of the King of Spain but those of twentieth-century London. He was roisterous, swaggering, cheerful, lovable, boastful and a pot-walloper. He was far more at home in a pub than in the Savoy Grill. If one half of him longed to swing a cutlass on the Spanish Main the other half of him was forever thumping pewter pots under the nose of Dr Johnson in the Cheshire Cheese.

Let me premise the tale of Tom Innes by saying straight away that he was a first-class journalist. He could sniff out news like a terrier. He could 'think big' on matters of high politics. Also he had an innate love of English literature. He could quote the classics by the hour and roar out resounding poetry with the éclat of a Belloc or a Chesterton. He has a vast knowledge of Elizabethan history and he read every tale of pirates and highwaymen that he could lay his hands on. The unquenchable boy lurked beneath the unquenchable thirst.

His staff loved him. Any reporter whom Tommy Innes sent out on a story left the office with a high flame in his heart. Tom inspired the crusading spirit and gave a buccaneering flavour to the production of each edition. Life to him was always a high adventure, to be celebrated with gallons of ale and the roaring of songs.

There was more than one occasion when, in between putting editions to bed he would sally forth into Fleet Street, storm into one of his favourite pubs, followed by his little devoted band of reporters and feature-writers and, at the drop of a hat clear the bar with the leg of a chair. This does not mean that he was guilty of physical assault or that he was a bully or a mere brawler in taverns. He was merely enacting the latest Regency rake or Elizabethan ruffler who happened to be dwelling in his mind at the moment. Tom Innes's rows were always good-natured rows. He was nobody's enemy but his own.

There was the famous occasion however, when, for once he was physically bested. Castlerosse announced his engagement to that fashionable lady of many lovers of whom Beaverbrook thoroughly disapproved. Innes sitting at the editorial desk said in front of the assembled heads of staff, 'Good God, Valentine! Why buy the book when you can get the damn thing from the library?'

Castlerosse, without a word, strode across the room, picked up the bulky editor from his chair, poised him for a moment in his arms and dropped him with a resounding crash into his own wastepaper basket. It split to atoms.

Beaverbrook said to me when he appointed me General Manager of the *Sunday Express,* 'You have two great and difficult tasks to perform. The first is to persuade my good friend Mr Selfridge to drop that stupid contract which I lost to him on the toss of a coin whereby he gets a full page of the *Sunday Express* for a year at a cut price. The second task is to get Tom Innes off the booze. That will be your most difficult assignment.' It was. I succeeded with Selfridge, but never with Innes.

This is not to say that Tom Innes was not a superb journalist. He knew the craft from A to Z. He could have gone out as a reporter and done as good a job as any man on his staff. He was a first-class sub-editor with a genius for writing arresting headlines. Moreover, he wrote careful and good English. There was none of the modern slip-shod Americanese or tortured English which debases too many popular newspapers today. I can think of many slick young Fleet Street journalists who, at this moment, would not survive for a second under Tom Innes or, for that matter, R.D.B.

Innes raised the literary side of the *Sunday Express* to hitherto undreamt heights. Not only did Arnold Bennett, H. G. Wells, Bernard Shaw and many prominent statesmen and politicians contribute to the paper but Tom trained young men on his own staff to become notable writers.

Anthony Praga, son of the gentle, erudite miniature-painter Alfred Praga who had married into the courtly family of Knollys was a case in point. Tony was the only Roman Catholic Jew with an Irish mother that I have ever come across. He could write with the pen of a poet but he could not tell the time. His copy was invariably late. His knowledge of the classics, on the other hand, was profound. Therefore Tom Innes suggested that he should blend his poetic pen with his classic background and produce a series to be called 'Love Stories of the Great'. In it Praga told in tender, moving English, without the slightest suspicion of mawkish sentiment, the love stories of gods and goddesses of the Grecian past, the romances of medieval chivalry and eighteenth-century elegance. It was not solely journalism. It was literature. Had Praga been a business man the book rights alone would have insured him a comfortable income for life. Alas, he died in poverty, years later.

Then there was that unbelievable man with the unbelievable name, Nathanial Gubbins. He began life, I believe, as a sort of office boy or librarian's assistant in the *Daily Express* library, that bewildering catacomb of carefully filed and docketed newspaper cuttings, reports, confidential documents and reference books which hold the keys to a thousand avenues of knowledge and news.

He longed to be a reporter. I believe I am right in saying that he first came to Beaverbrook's notice when, as a young reporter, he was sent down to Burwash in Sussex to interview Rudyard Kipling. It was a forlorn hope as Kipling prized his privacy. Gubbins was turned back either at the lodge-keeper's cottage or at the front door. Disconsolately he wandered on foot up a country lane of dog-roses and honeysuckle. An old roadmender was sitting on a pile of stones eating his midday bread and cheese. Gubbins, downcast by his abortive mission, greeted the old man with that mournful bloodhound look of his and said, 'I suppose you never see Mr Kipling do you?' And by the grace of God which looks after young journalists, the old roadmender opened up like a flower. Many a talk he and Kipling had had together. Mrs Kipling was as a sister unto the old man. Nat Gubbins listened, both ears cocked, his mind registering each phrase and memory.

The result, when he got back to the office, was a moving column of highly readable journalism. The roadmender's view on the Kipling menage were far more entrancing than any mere straightforward interview could ever have been. Beaverbrook, who read every line in his newspapers – and most of the lines in other newspapers – spotted the innate promise of the unknown young reporter. He rang the office for him right away. Nat Gubbins had his first foot on the rung of the ladder.

Later, when John Gordon became editor of the *Sunday Express* in succession to Tom Innes who had joined Herbert Wilcox's film company at an astronomic salary – and alas, later died in poverty – Gordon gave Gubbins his first leg up the ladder of humorous journalism – the comic column.

Gubbins who had, as I have said, a lugubrious countenance and a solemn pair of owl-eyes, was not, to look at, a humourist. But at various office dinners and functions, he had made his comic mark by inditing highly diverting fake telegrams from such people as the deposed Kaiser Wilhelm of Germany, the Archbishop of Canterbury, George Robey the comedian, Aimee MacPherson the American revivalist, the Keeper of the Privy Purse and others of equal fame who were totally unaware of the ribald messages sent in their names.

'If you can write this sort of stuff,' John Gordon said, 'you can write a comic column. We need one. Make the readers laugh. Beachcomber does it in the *Daily Express*. You can do it in the *Sunday Express*.'

Thus was born the famous Nathanial Gubbins column. It was written literally with blood, sweat and tears. Gubbins produced each joke as the laboured result of a journalistic Caesarian operation. Like so many good writers he wrote with difficulty. The result was brilliant. There had never been another Gubbins.

Another budding writer to whom Tom Innes and R.D.B. both

gave free rein and immense inspiration was my old friend and colleague, Jimmy Wentworth Day, who has since written 43 books and edited a number of glossy journals. He began as Publicity Manager after learning the rudiments of journalism on the Cambridge *Daily News*, where he also did an extra-mural course in English Literature at the university. From there he graduated to the composing room where he 'made-up' both the *Sunday* and *Daily Express* six nights a week and then turned to serious feature writing. The result was a series of articles which included the memoirs of such notable characters as the Earl of Rosslyn, one of the greatest gamblers of the period; Joe Cannon, the 'Father of the Turf' among racehorse trainers; the exploits of the fabulous Major-General 'One Arm' Sutton, the English adventurer who ruled half China with a succession of private armies; Trader Horn, an incredible old man who suddenly emerged from the hinterland of the Congo with unbelievable stories of hidden treasure, pagan rites and a mysterious white goddess who held court in a temple of skulls; together with the memoirs of such people of the times as Charles B. Cochran, the greatest producer of light musicals of this century; and a host of sporting celebrities.

The result of these trained young writers acting under an inspiring editor was that the paper never had a dull page in it. It was always lively, entertaining and out-of-the-rut.

Then came the era of John Gordon, the tall, dour, deliberate, black-haired, pale-faced Scot from Aberdeen with a rakish muscular figure and a fierce pride in the fact that he was a 'working journalist'. So, for that matter, were they all. R.D.B., the supreme head of affairs, could set up a column of type himself as good as that of any trade union Linotype operator.

John Gordon is one of the most experienced newspaper-men in active circulation. Above all, he is the supreme personal columnist. John's weekly column in the *Sunday Express* is one of the most widely read – and widely feared – features of Sunday journalism. He does not hesitate to expose abuses, ridicule excesses, pinpoint scandal or lay bare fraud. Like Beaverbrook, he had a Presbyterian upbringing. This almost Calvinist sense of right and wrong, of moral values and financial probity colours his whole outlook. That is why he is the terror of the apostles of the loose permissiveness of recent years.

Time and again John has attacked filth in the Press, filth on the stage, filth on TV and filth in books. He not only stirs up the mud, but he pours his own harsh disinfectant of ridicule upon the purveyors of mud. For this we can be grateful.

Journalism exists not only to disseminate news and express views, but to expose and damn fraud, crime, obscenity, hypocrisy and perversion. John Gordon is the enemy of these things.

I can perhaps best express the sort of 'intellectual' rubbish of which he is the constant enemy if I reprint this from a piece by Peter Simple, the corrosive columnist of the *Daily Telegraph*. He quotes the following rubbish:

' "All but a handful of fanatics, Irish earls or dowager ladies, with ample private means and time on their hands, now recognize that the great mass of people are not unduly concerned one way or the other, over 'charters for queers', four-letter words, nudes, profanity or dirty postcards, so long as checks are kept on prices and unemployment."

'This passage comes from the Annual Report of the National Secular Society, whose "Distinguished Members' Panel" (sic) includes Michael Foot, M.P., Brigid Brophy, Baroness Wootton, Lord Willis and George Melly.'

It is precisely that sort of half-baked thinking which John Gordon derides and attacks. He does a great public service.

We who run popular daily and Sunday newspapers know well that the average working-class and middle-class family in this country still have their strict codes of moral values and decent behaviour. They may enjoy a dirty joke or a bawdy song or revel in the police-court reports, but when dirt for dirt's sake is elevated to a so-called intellectual level, the ordinary reader welcomes the man who can prick the pretentious bubble and expose the hot air which it contains.

That is why John Gordon has an immense readership for his column. That is why he is feared by those who try to make quick, slick, fortunes out of filthy plays, blue films, four-letter books and the rest of the gutter-garbage which has bubbled to the top like scum in the last few years.

One remembers with sardonic relish the John Gordon Club – and its very short life. This was formed by Graham Greene, the novelist, and John Sutro, the film producer, to 'tease' John after he had denounced in his column Graham Greene's fulsome praise of Vladimir Nabokov's *Lolita*, which, as you will remember, dealt with a teenage nymphomaniac and her exploits. Greene picked it as one of his three favourite books of the year although at that time it was practically unknown on the bookstalls in London and New York. John condemned Greene's praise of the book as 'prurient', which my Oxford Dictionary tells me means 'Given to indulgence of lewd ideas,' or 'Having morbid desire or curiosity'. So now we know what John thought about Mr Graham Greene and his praise of *Lolita*. The result, as I have said, was the formation of the John Gordon Club as a 'Tease on John Gordon', as Mr Sutro expressed it.

They decided to hold a public meeting to discuss the morality or immorality of *Lolita*. John Gordon promised to be there. He may attack others, but he never runs away from attack on himself. The meeting was held in a private room in the Horseshoes Hotel in Tottenham Court Road on a suffocatingly hot night. Those on the platform, apart from John, were Graham Greene, John Sutro and A. S. Frere of Heinemanns, the publisher. Randolph Churchill, sweating like a pig in his shirtsleeves, was in the audience to report the meeting for the *Evening Standard*. As one might expect, Randolph disregarded the fact that he was on our staff – for the evening at any rate – and stood up and harangued everybody and anybody with blistering eloquence. When one woman objected, he said in a voice of thunder, 'Madam, if you continue in this way I shall have you removed.'

Anita Loos, who was there with Lilian Gish, the film star, said afterwards that it was the most uproariously amusing evening either of them had ever known. John Gordon more than held his own. When his column appeared the following Sunday he wiped the floor with the so-called 'intellectuals'.

Thus, in an odd way, John Gordon the Puritan crusader had achieved precisely what James Douglas had achieved twenty years or more before when he attacked *The Well of Loneliness*. Both set out to damn a grubby book. Both succeeded in boosting its sale to hitherto unheard of heights. So although the John Gordon Club had a short life, it had the last laugh.

John Gordon is today by far the richest 'working journalist' in Fleet Street. It would not surprise me if he is worth half a million. In fact, Jimmy Wentworth Day, who knows a lot about land and agriculture, tells me that John asked him some years ago if he (Jimmy) could recommend a good landed property which John could buy as an investment. Jimmy, thinking that he wanted to buy a 'hobby farm' of perhaps fifty acres for perhaps £20,000, asked, 'How much money do you want to invest?'

'Oh, about a quarter of a million,' John replied blandly: And he meant it. Obviously John, being a shrewd business man, knew that the scale of death duties on agricultural land is much lower than that on stocks and shares. John, like the rest of us, has no love for Mr Bloodsucker, the tax man.

One may well ask how he has made what is generally regarded in Fleet Street as an immense fortune, out of his earnings as a journalist. After all, he began as a penniless youth on a newspaper in Dundee, the granite-faced city which has nurtured some of the most successful journalistic freebooters who ever came South to snap up the plum jobs in Fleet Street. John may have earned his £5,000 or £10,000 as an editor with generous expenses – but how does that add up to the presumed half million? Or even the declared quarter of a million? I ask, not out of envy, but out of admiration.

The answer, I believe, lies in his genius for investing his earnings in insurance and annuities and then reinsuring and buying fresh annuities when the old ones fall in. He got the idea of buying annuities from an old friend of mine who was the London General Manager of a famous insurance company.

John's habits – and since he writes a lot about other people's habits he must not blame me if I expose his – are a mixture of parsimony and luxury. He has dwelt for many years in a tall detached Victorian house in Addiscombe Road, Croydon. The sort of house which well-to-do city merchants lived in when the whole area was countryfied suburbia. Then, as bricks and mortar advanced, the value declined a bit. I believe John took it originally on lease at thirty shillings week. He has lived there ever since. Today he owns it.

In those early working days he went up to Fleet Street by train and bus. For the last twenty years or so he has done the journey by Rolls-Royce, which he always drives himself. John loves his Rolls as other men love their pet girl-friends. Whether he has any of those or not I have yet to discover.

He has lunch frequently at the Press Club where the menu is cheap enough to satisfy even a Scot. There he meets his old friends, plays a game of billiards, chuckles when he wins and then stalks out smoking the longest cigar in Fleet Street.

Those cigars are not only long, but highly expensive. Listen to the tale.

I met John stalking up Fleet Street one sunny Monday morning. Now Monday is the universal day off for all Sunday-paper workers. It is their equivalent of the normal man's Saturday. So I asked him, 'What on earth are you doing in the Street on a Monday?'

'I'm off to draw my Old Age Pension.'

'Old Age Pension!' I spluttered. 'You ought to be ashamed of yourself drawing money from the State with all your money to burn. You must have the biggest banking account of any journalist I know. What on earth do you want the pension for?'

'I give it to my favourite charity,' John replied.

With visions of a printer's orphanage or a home for decayed journalists benefiting by stealth I relented and enquired, 'What is your favourite charity?'

'My cigars. I like the best. If I let my Old Age Pension mount up for a few weeks it buys a box of the best.'

Lest I do my old friend an injustice by quoting his wry witticism at his own expense I hasten to add that during his year of office as Chairman of the Newspaper Press Fund, Fleet Street's principal professional charity, the receipt of money in subscriptions and donations soared to a record height. John worked like a beaver to rake in the shekels for his less fortunate fellow-workers. I wonder how many who each Sunday read the dry wit, sharp criticism, penetrating investigations and fighting words of John Gordon realise that this up-to-the-minute, 'with-it' writer who is not only abreast of the times but often ahead of them is eighty-one.

On John's eightieth birthday Sir Max Aitken as Chairman of Beaverbrook Newspapers gave him a splendid birthday feast Several hundred people, eminent in politics, finance, commerce, advertising, literature and journalism turned up to pay homage to the master columnist.

When, before the function, John was asked where he would like it to be held, it was thought that he would inevitably pick his old haunt of other days, the Savoy Hotel. Not a bit of it. With his eye on a fitting national frame to set off the Gordon countenance, he replied brightly, 'the Banqueting House in Whitehall' which was built by Inigo Jones as the magnificent prelude to a far more magnificent palace which was never built. The Macmillan Government spent tens of thousands on restoring it to its pristine glory. I do not know if John based his choice on the fact that Charles I, the Stuart king, went from that hall to his execution on the scaffold, but I am quite certain that he is the only journalist who has ever been dined and wined in such glorious surroundings, attended by such illustrious company. Certainly he is the only one who has been presented by his proprietor at his birthday dinner with the key of a brand-new Rolls-Royce which was waiting outside for him at the door. At the end of it all, amid a roar of cheers, the one-time penniless boy-reporter from Dundee drove off in his glittering chariot to his Victorian suburban mansion at Croydon.

There he still dwells, the 'working journalist' who is never late on the job, never lacks the right word, never loses his friends, and never fails to create fresh enemies. Long life to him.

CHAPTER SEVEN

The Second World War

The Cabinet Minister and the Ghost of the Black Prince – J. H. Thomas's Story – Bombed out and Burnt out – 'A Hideous Shape' in Fleet Street by Night – Death Missed by Inches – The Comic Epic Of the American Home Guard – 'The Piccadilly Cowboys' – Rounding up a Tycoon with a Bayonet – Beaverbrook as Lord Privy Seal – I Am Summoned to the Seat of Power – 'Is Christiansen a Sound Man?' – Dramatic Death of 'Chris' – The Man Who Ran Away with Lord Beaverbrook under His Arm.

I was playing golf within sight and sound of the Sussex sea near Littlehampton on Sunday, September 3rd, 1939, a day of mellow sunshine, with George Allison, a well-known Fleet Street type, who was also a notable broadcaster and manager of the Arsenal Football Club. George was a genial chap and we were both looking forward to the nineteenth hole at the clubhouse.

Suddenly a woman, whom we did not know, came running down her garden path, which adjoined the golf course, and screaming excitedly: 'We're at war! The Prime Minister, Mr Chamberlain, has just announced on the wireless that Hitler has refused to accept Britain's terms, so war has been declared. Isn't it awful? '

My heart sank. Suddenly I was cold. Here it was, all over again. In 1914 as a youngster I had pulled every string to get into the army. Like thousands of others I had gone to war with high hopes and a bawdy song on my lips. Now I felt afraid. When you have once had a dose of war with all its death and stench and horrors, you don't run after it the second time unless you are a hero – or a fool. George and I looked at each other gloomily. The clubhouse was a long way off, so we decided to play on. We had no heart in the game. I foozled shot after shot. George was no better. The sparkle had gone out of life. We looked at each other and with one voice said, 'Let's pack it up.' The nineteenth hole beckoned.

As we were striding across the golf course the air raid sirens went. 'My God,' I thought, 'the Germans are on the ball – as usual. Not a moment wasted. Any minute now we'll catch a packet.' I searched the sky for the incoming wave of bombers, sweeping over the Channel, loaded with death. Not a sign. Not a buzz. It was, as we found out later, a false alarm.

We got to the clubhouse which was empty and had a sad, solitary drink, depressed in mind and body.

The last time I had been in that club, that cheerful chap, the late J. H. Thomas, one time Cabinet Minister, the most engaging and likeable man that the Socialist Party ever produced, had been there. Jim Thomas, who began life as an errand-boy, became an engine-driver and later Lord Privy Seal and Secretary of State for the Dominions with half an alphabet of honours after his name, was a lively, lovable, human being, a wag, a bon-viveur and the last Socialist on earth to dream of upsetting the Constitution or ruining a bottle of wine. He almost persuaded one to vote Labour. He was one of the best story-tellers ever let loose and was a constant joy to the late King George V who collected his jokes as other men collect rare cameos.

So, on that gloomy day of the Second World War, I thought of the occasion not long before when I had been playing golf on the same course with Stanley Bell, my old chum, who was Managing Director of the *Daily Mail*.

A storm of rain swept the course, ruined our game and drove us indoors. The clubhouse was deserted, so we marched into the bar, determined to have one drink only and clear off. There, by the grace of God, sat the Rt. Hon. James Henry Thomas, P.C., with a bottle of champagne in front of him and an expansive grin on his face.

'Come and join me, boys,' he said cheerfully. 'Let's make the best of a bad day. Steward, bring another bottle, please.' Who could resist such eloquence?

We sat down. For the next three-quarters of an hour he told story after story. Stanley Bell and I rocked with laughter. I positively ached. The stories were so good that I had no time to remember them. One of the minor tragedies of life. Then I got up to go. I said, 'Mr Thomas, I can't thank you enough for your hospitality and, what's more, for your stories. You're the best story-teller I've ever had the pleasure of listening to. You have

Some of those at my dinner for 'Fathers and Fighting Sons'. *l.* to *r.*:
Bill Duck's son; A. N. Other (back view); the inimitable Bob Foster;
Arthur Christiansen, Editor of the *Daily Express*; and my son Peter

'The Thirty Thieves': Members of the exclusive 'Thirty Club' of
advertising executives at their annual Christmas Fancy Dress Party

Above: An Unholy
Trinity. *l.* to *r.* Charles
Tomkinson, director
of the London Press
Exchange; Lord
Robens, then head of
the Coal Board; and
the author

Right: An historic
chimney-piece made
from wooden remains
of the bombed
Guildhall of London,
presented to the
Advertising Club of
New York. LWN on
right presenting the
finished piece to the
Chairman of the
Advertising Club

the gift of making every situation and every character real. *What a raconteur!*' Stanley Bell nodded agreement.

Jim Thomas put out his hand as we were about to leave and said, 'Thank you for those kind words. I do appreciate them enormously. But before you go, let me tell you the true story of when I wasn't the shiny boy of the hour – in other words, I tripped up badly.' We sat down to listen expectantly.

'You compliment me on being a raconteur,' he said. 'But I can tell you an occasion when I had a great disappointment. I had one ambition, and that was to become a member of a certain club where the qualification was to tell an original funny story.' And he went on to say: 'It was my ambition to be a member of the Duncannon Literary Society and the qualification necessary was to stand up at the annual dinner and tell an original funny story. As you kindly said, I have a good repertoire of stories. I got up and proceeded with what I thought to be an unique episode in my life until a member called, "Chestnut!" I started on another story and another member interrupted, "The story you are telling has got whiskers on it." I wilted. As I started on my third story the Secretary of the Society said, "You're about to tell a story that was included in the records of this Honourable Company in the year 1895."'

Mr Thomas said to us, 'It shook me. My membership seemed to be going out of the window.' So he racked his brains and, dropping his aitches, which he often did, he said, 'It is my usual 'abit of a hevening when I've come out of the 'Ouse to walk acrorst to Westminster Habbey. I usually go to a quiet spot where I think about my life and my duties in the 'Ouse. I went on to say that I was sitting in the chapel in the Habbey when I 'ears a voice address me and say, "Turn me over, Thomas," Acrorst the little chapel I sees the heffigy of the Black Prince, the great 'ero of the Middle Ages.

'I said, "Is that you, Yer Royal 'Ighness?" And the voice came back, 'Aye, it is I, Thomas. Turn me over." So I said to 'Is Royal 'Ighness, 'Your request is my command, but why do you want to be turned over?"

'And the voice said, "So that the members of the Duncannon Literary Society can kiss my backside!" I was helected!'

I'm afraid that it was at that point we had another bottle.

I was cheered by the memory of Jim Thomas's story when I returned after September 3rd to find the usually ebullient *Daily Express* atmosphere of self-confidence a little tattered. Not surprising. For weeks past our lord and master, the Beaver, had been declaring by word of mouth, in headlines an inch high and on newspaper placards throughout the country: THERE WILL BE NO WAR. Alas, for once he was wrong. Knowing the sincerity of the man I have often wondered what was behind it. Was it propaganda? Did he honestly believe it? He was too much of a realist to indulge in wishful thinking. What was the truth behind that highly publicized declaration of optimism which, for once in his life, made him look a fool? Shall we ever know?

The *Daily Express* promptly set up a realistc policy of air raid precautions, warnings and fire watchers. Whereas most other offices employed outsiders to keep watch the *Daily Express* put its three available Directors on the roof to do round-the-clock sentry-go. Their job was to warn the rest of the staff throughout the building of approaching enemy aircraft or of any outbreaks of fire caused by nearby bomb explosions or incendiary bombs on the building itself. The moment the alarm was given all employees were expected to down tools and go straight down to the machine room in the bowels of the earth, the roof of which was supported by massive concrete pillars. It was far safer than the average dug-out.

This meant that E. J. Robertson and myself and one other Director each did a minimum twenty-four hour stint of watching on the roof, high above most of the roofs of London with a bird's eye view of Fleet Street at our feet. Our original shelter, exposed to all the winds that blew, was a rickety wooden hut over the top of the lift shaft – not an ideal sentry-box since a nearby explosion might have tipped one down the lift shaft, a sheer fall of well over a hundred feet. Later we were given a more substantial shelter with no hole in the floor.

Apart from the fact that it is always good for morale for a commander in war to take as great, or greater, risks than his men this policy of picking Directors as roof-watchers had a practical side to it. Each of us knew the printing time of each edition of the paper to the minute. We knew the precise time which would be allotted to the packaging, loading and despatch of the bundles of newspapers. We knew the times at which the mail trains would leave London to take the newspapers north, south, east and west. Come what might, we were determined that the *Express*, short of total destruction, would always be printed and would always get through. It did.

There was plenty of excitement. Bombs fell all round us. London, for a period, endured fires in some area or another almost each night of the week. It was always a toss-up whether the next bomb would be ours. One bomb did hit the *Daily Express* building. Fortunately it was not a blockbuster which would have blown the entire premises, old and new, to bits. But it did set fire to the old wooden-floored and largely wooden-walled original offices with one entrance at 8 Shoe Lane and another at 23 St Bride's Street. There Lord Beaverbrook had his private flat perched like an eagle's nest on top of the building. It was burnt out from top to bottom. Luckily the Beaver was not in his nest – or should it not be 'lodge'? The bomb fell on a Sunday night.

One got used to standing up there alone under the stars in blacked-out London, the night sky seared by searchlights, the black-out rent by occasional flashes as bombs exploded and by leaping tongues of flames when buildings were set ablaze. Odd bits of old iron including our own anti-aircraft shells and shrapnel, sang past one's ears. It was no man's land all over again – with a difference. This time we were not flat on our belly's as Robbie and I had so often been in the mud of Flanders, but we were high up and alarmingly exposed.

One great advantage of having an entirely volunteer force of look-outs and fire watchers was that with intimate knowledge of our own printing procedure we could usually allow an extra two or three minutes for the presses to thunder on before giving the alarm. Other newspaper offices which employed professional roof-spotters who were not versed in the techniques of newspaper production, usually gave their alarms several minutes before the actual deadline of necessity. Two or three minutes in the high-speed production of a newspaper can mean a lot.

One night a somewhat self-important member of the staff took the trouble to come all the way up in the lift to complain to me that he and some of his colleagues did not think that we were giving sufficient time before sounding the alarm.

I invited him on to the roof and directing him to the various points of the compass said, 'You know we *are* experienced in this sort of thing. We've had plenty of practice. If aircraft are coming from *that* direction it means that they are heading for the centre of London. In that case we sound the alarm instantly. If, on the other hand, aircraft are heading in *that* other direction – or over there – we know that they are going to give the London area a miss. As for doodle-bugs (flying bombs) we can tell from their trail of fire precisely which way they are going. They never veer off course.'

Our complainant digested these facts slowly. Then, as the winter wind nipped him with a miserly grip in his kidneys, shivered and said, 'Damn cold up here. Pretty lonely too.'

'Not always lonely,' I replied. 'We often get a shell nose-cap or a load of shrapnel buzzing round our ears.' At that moment the sirens went. He shivered with apprehension.

'Better stay up here and see the fun,' I suggested genially. 'Then you'll be able to report back on how we plot the directions of incoming enemy aircraft. Nothing like seeing for yourself.'

'I must be getting back to the lads,' he announced hurriedly. 'They'll be waiting for me to report.' And he was down the lift shaft like a ferret down a rabbit hole.

The most dramatic moment of all came silently, unexpectedly. Strube, that brilliant cartoonist, stepped out of the front door into Fleet Street to take his usual taxi back to his home in Golders Green.

In the half light of the stars and a dim moon he saw, in the middle of Fleet Street, only just above or on the surface of the road, a hideous oblong metal shape attached to a parachute which had wrapped itself round the overhead power cables of the street lights. One cable had snapped with the result that the oblong had fallen on its side and not on its nose. Had it done so the entire *Daily Express* office would have been blown to rubble.

Strube shot back into the office like a scalded cat, shouting, 'Good God! There's a landmine out in the street within a couple of yards of the front door.'

The staff laughed at him. When they went to the door and saw it was true their faces were parchment. The building was vacated within minutes and we all left for the *Evening Standard* office at the other end of Shoe Lane.

Shortly afterwards those double-dyed heroes, The Bomb Disposal Squad, arrived. Those men took their lives in their hands every minute of their working hours. The mine was defused and taken away. Any reader who has seen the fearful devastation which can be caused by a landmine will know precisely what Fleet Street missed that night. Not only would the *Daily Express* building have been destroyed but half the rest of the Street would have been either demolished or badly damaged. So far as the London Press was concerned it was the nearest squeak of the war.

The British have their own odd ways of expressing, in their own unwarlike way, their contempt for the dangers of war. So it was with the *Daily Express*. A 'rest room' was allocated to our little squad of roof-watchers. It had beds, chairs and tables. There one was supposed to have a peaceful nap to break the monotony of the 24-hour watch. This rest room was on the top floor!

Luckily, I personally could offset the midnight rigours of roof-spotting with the lighter diversions of the American Home Guard whose battlefield was the West End. Other people joined the British Home Guard which, nicknamed 'Dad's Army' or 'The Rag-Time Field Force', none the less did a sterling job and would no doubt have given the Germans something to think about had they landed. They may have been unmilitary in demeanour and possibly pot-bellied in appearance but, by and large, they were men of spirit who although middle-aged or downright elderly, turned out, wet or fine, with rifles and bayonets, packs and trenching tools to defend England to the last beach, the last hedge and the last ditch.

I was at that time, and still am, a member of that jolly institution, the American Club which has its clubhouse in Piccadilly. So, with one or two other Britons, I joined the American Home Guard which was the brain-child of Brigadier General Wade Hayes, an ex-officer of the First World War who had been on General Pershing's staff at American Army H.Q.

This particular Home Guard numbered about fifty convivial, bibulous but none the less dedicated souls. We were sworn to defend the last cocktail bar, the last pub and the last nightclub in the West End. Our headquarters were in Buckingham Gate and our chosen duty was to furnish a guard of eight armed men each night at Leconfield House in Curzon Street which was then the H.Q. of London Command. I have often wondered if the brass-hats realized the perils to which they were exposed!

This was no ordinary Home Guard. There had never been one like it before and I doubt if there will ever be one like it again. With the exception of us few Britons the rest were all American business men. Park Lane and Piccadilly were the chosen battlefront of the gold-plated cowboys.

We were supposed to be highly mobile and were described as troopers. We had no horses but we had eight Packard motorcars, supplied by gilded Americans. Luckily we did not wear spurs. We were armed with tommy-guns straight from Chicago. When we went to Bisley rifle ranges once a month for musketry practice it is said that we fired off more ammunition in one afternoon than the whole Brigade of Guards discharged in a week. When we went to Sunningdale for field exercises we were accompanied by a large Ford van. This was the field commissariat. It contained such Spartan 'iron rations' as champagne, crates of whisky and choice sandwiches.

An eminent trooper, who shall be nameless, was so portly that it would have been downright cruelty to send him on field exercises. So he was left behind with a loaded rifle to guard the motor-cars and the 'canteen', whilst the rest of us went off to wallow in bogs, get scratched by gorse, crawl in the heather and be bitten by adders and horse-flies.

One had only to cast one's eye backwards when marching off to observe the portly trooper fish out his cigar case, light up a king-size Larranaga, produce his flask, cock his leg in comfort and settle back to a philosophical contemplation of the horrors of war with his rifle uncocked and 'at the easy'.

Now let me tell the odd tale of how I came to join this select body of the elect. I was aware that many of my comrades-in-arms were very important advertisers. Therefore it seemed good business to keep an eye on them in war. I went down with a few friends from the American Club and we were sworn-in in the American style, giving the oaths with our hats across our chests. When I returned the next day in uniform I had my M.C. ribbon and battle honours on my tunic. This surprised the general as I was the only one who had seen battle service. He immediately came up to me and invited me to lunch at the Savoy the next day. This was a very pleasant surprise, and I duly accepted. He said, 'Needham, you are now a member of the American Home Guard and I see that you have had service before, so I am going to make you a Lootenant.'

The next time I went on parade I had the two pips on my shoulder. I was regarded as a cad. Promotion within 24 hours was not playing the game I was given command of the awkward squad, composed chiefly of my friends, especially my business 'friends'.

This brings me to the 'mutiny' of that redoubtable fellow, the late Bob Foster, the head of the immensely rich American Colgate-Palmolive Company in Britain. He was a tall, thin, gaunt chap with steely eyes, a hawk nose and an unfathomable capacity for dry martinis. The only part of soldiering which appealed to him was marching round and round the drill hall. He was largely a stranger to fresh air.

Came the occasion when there was to be a surprise mustering of all Home Guards in the country to repel a mock German invasion. Brigadier General Wade Hayes was determined that the American Home Guard, was to be the first on parade. Trooper Foster was dining out that particular night at the Mirabelle with another member of the Home Guard, Trooper Drucker, who was Managing Director of the Ever-ready Razor Company when the message came through that Trooper Foster and Trooper Drucker, who were entertaining two ladies, were to be on parade *at once.*

They had already been warned to expect the call. Both refused to cut their dinner short. Eventually they arrived at headquarters, lurching slightly. They were greeted by General Wade Hayes who gave them an imperial rocket. To which they answered, 'Crap! We are going back to finish our dinner.'

This was too much for the general who sent for Lieutenant Needham, their troop commander. In my best military style I ordered them to get on parade immediately, 'and jump to it'. To which Foster replied, 'Hoss manure! Don't you b—— me about, Bill. I'll cancel that goddam advertising contract!' We're going back to finish our dinner.

It was time to show my authority. One could not clap them in irons, give them Field Punishment No. 1, or, worse luck, put them on the latrine squad. I made up my mind very quickly. As they were leaving the building, I put another private, who happened to be the hall porter of the American Embassy, on the door with a fixed bayonet to prevent them leaving the building. To which Trooper Foster said, 'Bullshit! You don't think that that bloody skewers' gonna stop us?' The trooper then lunged his bayonet at Foster's stomach.

Foster flinched at the bare steel just as Napoleon's Old Guard flinched before the British bayonets at Waterloo. Meekly he retreated to the bar upstairs to drown his disgrace. The ladies at the Mirabelle were left to wail and wait, the innocent casualties of war.

Foster's final fling of defiance as he stumbled upstairs to the bar was to invite me to perform an unnatural act upon myself. Such were the hazards of service with the American Home Guard.

Foster's son, incidentally, joined the English Air Force and received two medals for bravery at Buckingham Palace. He is now the executive President of the Colgate-Palmolive Company in America. The strain of the unquenchable Bob still flourishes.

Meanwhile our lord and master had been translated by the Prime Minister, Churchill, to the lofty office of Lord Privy Seal. This meant that he was no longer in active day-to-day command of his newspaper empire. We were to miss the constant telephonic spur. The flow of memos ceased. No longer was one summoned to the presence, in London or at Cherkley. But in spite of his new and exalted duty his heart and mind were still in Fleet Street.

Robertson, unfortunately, was ill. So I had to take his place. That made me temporarily the supreme boss, the man-in-charge on the spot. I was not allowed to forget it. There came a call from the Beaver to ask if I would be kind enough to go along and have a chat.

I set off to his new headquarters, Gwydyr House, a stately one-time private mansion of nobility, in Whitehall. I was, I confess, full of apprehension, more than a little suspicious. When the Beaver was in his kindliest mood and issued his most courteous invitation to come into his parlour one knew that he was at his most dangerous. He wanted to find out. He was suspicious of something or other. When he was in that mood his method of constant interrogation coupled with gentle insinuation and crowned by the sudden hammer-blow of a forthright statement or demand was the nearest thing to brain-washing I have ever been through. He would have made a superb Queen's Counsel. What, I wondered, was in the wind? And had he summoned Arthur Christiansen, the young, ebullient and somewhat bouncey editor? Chris was a good editor and he did not fail to let one know it.

I was ushered into a stately and lofty room on the first floor. 'The little man' was alone. No sign of Chris. He rose to his feet, stalked across the carpet, shook me warmly by the hand and said, 'I apologize for bringing you here. But you understand, Needham, that this is the only way I can keep in touch with my business.' Then, right out of the blue, he added, 'How do you get on with Christiansen?'

'Very well, sir.'

'You think he's doing a good job?'

'I do.'

'This,' he said, 'is very important, because I rely on you young men to keep the ship steady on its course – and you do believe that Christiansen is the right man for the job?'

'Undoubtedly,' I said.

'He's an emotional man, you know.' He went on. 'And so am I. But I have to rely on the business side, people like you to keep an even balance. Without people like you I obviously couldn't be doing the job I am doing for the country now.'

Then he suddenly demanded, 'Do you think Christiansen is a sound man?'

Perhaps without thinking I said, 'He's inclined to be a bit hysterical.'

'What do you mean?'

I spluttered a bit and tried to convey that what I really meant was that any editor of imagination was bound to be a little keyed-up on occasions. Beaverbrook was still looking doubtful, with his eyes fixed on me, obviously about to cross-examine me more sharply when, luckily, the telephone rang. It was an urgent call from the office to say that a mob of cranky demonstrators, of the sort with which we have become only too familiar, had swarmed into the front hall of the *Daily Express* and were kicking up a row. I was wanted at once to deal with them.

'Back to the office, Needham,' Beaverbrook said instantly. 'Whatever you do don't let those people stay in the front hall or get further into the building. Get 'em out.'

I left hurriedly, glad to escape the inquisition.

This was the beginning of the end of my long association with Arthur Christiansen although it was to be several years before he retired – or was retired – and plunged with tremendous enthusiasm into the film industry. He took a major part in a film entitled, I think, 'The Day that The Earth Caught Fire'. In spite of its title it was not a howling success. And Christiansen, although he took the part of a newspaper editor in the film showed unfortunately that he was no born film actor.

Soon after, he asked me to lunch at the Savoy. He was full of himself, bubbling with self-confidence. He asked me to help one of his sons who was in the advertising business which I gladly promised to do. Then he rushed off to catch a train to a film studio somewhere in the Eastern Counties. An hour or so later his wife telephoned me in a state of high distress to say that he had gone on to the film set and, in the full glare of the lights, dropped dead. He was only in his fifties. That was the dramatic end of the 'boy editor' who had made the liveliest impact on Fleet Street of any newcomer, between the two World Wars.

Talking of the *Daily Express* and the versatility of Lord Beaverbrook reminds me of a notable fact which is, I think, known to few people. Beaverbrook was the master-designer of his own building, that great glistening edifice of black and silver and glass which glitters like a gigantic cinema and is known to the irreverent as 'Lord Beaverbrook's Lavatory'. It was, in fact, his own brain child.

It had been decided, years before, to build a new office fronting Fleet Street. Partly on the site of the old offices and partly on the ground which had been occupied for so many years by that historic little journalists' hide out, 'The Sausage Shop', in which two old ladies served the most succulent sausages sizzling away in the front window with mountains of fried onions. Behind it was a small printing works owned by one jobbing printer. The two old ladies and the printer, although offered tantalizing prices, stubbornly refused to sell out. They were Naboth's Vineyard epitomized. Finally when an astronomic price was offered they gracefully accepted the cheques, folded their tents and stole silently away to gilt-edged retirement.

A new and stately façade in the traditional classic style of English architecture was planned. It was, by a very odd coincidence, precisely of the same style as the *Daily Telegraph* building of today. The *Telegraph,* however, had not showed its hand. When their new building went up, Beaverbrook was horrified to find that, having a much wider frontage to Fleet Street, the new *Daily Telegraph* would completely dwarf his proposed edifice and make it look like a downtrodden younger brother. That was unthinkable. So, having seen a few examples of ultra-modern Scandinavian architecture, he immediately sat down and drafted his own ideas of the sketches of a new building which, inspired by Scandinavia, was to look like nothing else Fleet Street had ever seen. It still looks that way.

He went further and personally designed the decorations and plans of the imposing front hall. That also is remarkable and eye-catching. In bas-relief are depicted in gold, silver and black the emblems of empire, of agriculture and of industry – all the things which were nearest to his heart. At the back of the broad sweep of shallow stairs which lead up to an inner lobby where the lifts go up and down a small sardonic bust of the old man his face wrinkled monkey-wise, shrewd eyes, questioning relentlessly, his mouth widened into the grin which every cartoonist called 'impish', sits for ever surveying the scene.

It had not been long in place, sitting snugly on its marble pillar, before a youngish, smartly-dressed man who looked like a barrister, walked into the front hall with a slight stagger, marched up the few steps to the bust, flung his arms round it, cuddled it to his bosom and then, finding it was movable, suddenly snatched it up.

He bolted out of the front hall into Fleet Street like a hare with Lord Beaverbrook under his arm! The whole corps of commissionaires with a flock of office boys leapt to their feet, poured out of the door, and chased the runaway thief like a pack of hounds. Their quarry, shouting with laughter, ran like a good 'un. They caught him in Ludgate Circus, a full two hundred yards from the office, still giggling and, highly pleased with himself. They marched the thief back to the office, took the bust from him, rang Robertson and reported the matter. Robbie, having a dry sense of Scots humour, saw the joke, came down with a magisterial air and told the man he had made a damn fool of himself.

Those of us who knew Robertson and his normally rather stern demeanour saw for a fleeting moment the flicker of a rare smile as he told the commissionaires to let the thief go.

The Man Who Stole Lord Beaverbrook walked out, slightly shamefaced, but still with a smirk. We shall never know his name. Today Lord Beaverbrook is screwed firmly down.

CHAPTER EIGHT

The New Beaverbrook Era

'The Young Master' Takes Over – Why Sir Max Aitken Is Not the Second Baron Beaverbrook – When Max Wanted Overtime Pay – Winston Churchill and Randolph – Max as A War Hero – His Quick Generosity – £10,000 for the Press Club – The Famous Swaffer Dinner Party – Lord Thomson's Historic Banquet – Beaverbrook's Farewell to Life.

Newspapers, like nations, have their ruling dynasties. Kings and empires come and go. The same applies to Press lords and their paper empires. Before Northcliffe died a new star, that of the young Max Aitken, M.P. for Ashton-under-Lyne, had blazed on the Fleet Street horizon. Today another young Max Aitken takes over the empire which his father, the redoubtable Beaverbrook, founded. I am lucky enough in my working life to have spanned both these great eras of these two dominant Press lords with a foot mid-way in the Rothermere kingdom.

Enough has been written about Lord Beaverbrook to fill a small library. Some who have written about him have done so eulogistically – particularly when he was alive. It was a brave man who would have dared the wrath of 'the little man.' Since he died there have been one or two books about him for which I have no great admiration. At least one seems to have been written in a would-be clever-clever vein of sardonic mockery. It is easy for jackals to yap when the old lion is dead. There is an old saying 'no man is a hero to his valet,' but some valets, or their equivalents, show themselves to be less than heroic when, after death, they not-so-politely bite the hand that fed them.

I was, if you like, a sort of business valet to Beaverbrook. With all modesty, few men were closer to him than R.D.B., E. J. Robertson, Castlerosse and myself. We knew him in all his moods. Those moods were as unpredictable as summer thunderstorms. They veered from the royal raging temper to the sudden tenderness of a devoted father and husband in tears.

I had the sharp edge of his tongue many times. Usually I deserved it. Then, suddenly the sweetness of his smile lit up that

impish face and the sun shone. One veered from 'my good boy
Needham' to the cold and withering 'that man Needham'.
Throughout it all, rain or shine, he remained to me a good
friend, an inspiring employer and, in a real sense, a hero. His
son has taken on a similar mantle of high individuality with his
own differences.

The average reader may wonder why the Hon. John William
Max Aitken, D.S.O., D.F.C., holder of the Czech War Cross,
day-time fighter pilot during the Battle of Britain, later commander of a night fighter squadron and, to top it all, Group
Captain commanding Strike Mosquito Wing in Norwegian waters
and later Conservative Member of Parliament for Holborn, son of
the first Baron Beaverbrook, is not himself known as Lord
Beaverbrook.

When Beaverbrook, then eighty-six, was seriously ill, a few
months before his death, I said to his son, more or less flippantly,
'I suppose that sooner or later I shall have to get used to calling
you my lord.'

Max looked at me very seriously and said; 'No, Bill. I shall
never take that title. My father earned it by his own merit in
the First World War. He deserved it. I don't. I shall never use it.
There is only one Beaverbrook.'

That is the measure of the genuine admiration and affection
of son for father. So today in the Beaverbrook organization
which to us older ones is still very much a family, Sir Max
Aitken – when he renounced his father's peerage, he found he
had to keep the baronetcy – is known as 'the young master'. He
explained to me that he could renounce the peerage because he
had no intention of taking his seat in the House of Lords as the
second Baron Beaverbrook; 'but,' he added, 'I can't renounce the
baronetcy, so you'll have to be content with calling me Sir Max.'
So today he is on easy terms of friendship with the older members of his staff as either Sir Max or Max, according to place
and circumstances.

It is often said that great men overshadow their sons. It has
been said of Randolph Churchill and of the present Lord Birken-
head, to name only two in this generation. I knew Randolph
casually as one of our star contributors. He was a brilliant

journalist, an even more brilliant speaker and he could be the rudest man in Britain. Beaverbrook liked him because in a sense he was another Castlerosse, another form of court jester.

Those who knew father and son knew that there was a great affection and understanding between Winston and Randolph. Equally it was the general opinion that although Randolph worshipped his father, his repeated failures to get into Parliament – he contested several seats and was returned only once during an unopposed election – forced on him the bitter realization that he would never take on his father's mantle in the affairs of state. He took to journalism as the next best thing.

One could not say the same thing about old Max and young Max. Father and son had the same deep affinity and understanding as the two Churchills. But the son was never overshadowed by the father. Like his father he carved out his own distinguished career as a young man, not in the turmoil of the warfare of the Press, but in the far more dangerous warfare of the air. Since then he has taken over the reins of his remarkable father with a sure sense of guidance and leadership.

I first knew 'the young master' when he was an undergraduate at Pembroke College, Cambridge. I did not meet him at the university but I have a vivid memory of his first entry into the *Daily Express* office, during the Long Vacation, as a learner Linotype operator.

There he was in the din and clatter of the machine-room tapping away at his tall machine, in an inferno of noise, whilst the little bars of hot type metal fell into their container. I do not know whether his father suggested, as he might well have done, that the boy should start at the bottom, but at any rate, Sidney Long, the Superintendent of our mechanical side, was asked to find him something useful to do.

There he was sitting at his machine in the long line of skilled operators, tapping away with the slow deliberation of a beginner when the great Sidney Long came bustling along. Young Max turned to him and asked, 'Please, Mr Long, may I do some overtime tonight?'

'Oh no, Max,' said Sidney importantly. 'You don't have to do overtime. What put that idea into your head? Why do you want to do it?'

'Because I could do with the money,' young Max said simply. He got his overtime and his extra pay.

I don't know if he would have gone on to learn other basic elements of journalism and newspaper production. The chances are that he would not have missed a trick either as Linotype operator or junior reporter. Anyway, the Second World War burst upon us and in no time young Max Aitken who had already joined the Royal Auxiliary Air Force at the age of 16, four years previously, was in the front line of battle as a fighter pilot in the Battle of Britain when men were shot down in flames like flies and the fate of this country was decided in the air over Kent and Sussex. Flying appealed to his sense of adventure from those early schoolboy days. The love of it is with him still. He loves speed, the spice of danger, the thrill of combat and the risks which go with it.

He was a war hero in the true sense. I shall never forget the proud look on Lord Beaverbrook's face when his son came home on short leave from one of his many air battles. The Old Man put his arm round his boy's shoulders, gave him a hug of affection and said quietly, 'My brave boy.'

In those years young Max in the incredible stress of constant air warfare carved out his own strong personality for himself. Today he combines the resolution and determination of his father with the sweetness of his mother. Like the Old Man he cannot tolerate fools gladly but he is, of all the men I know, the most generous. I could tell many tales of young Max's heroism in war. If I did he might never speak to me again. He hates that sort of thing.

But I am going to tell one story about him, whether he likes it or not, which illustrates his spontaneous generosity. A certain well-known writer and one-time editor had left the *Daily Express* staff for some years when I heard by chance that he had fallen on very difficult times, was without a job, desperately ill and in the London Clinic, which is not the least expensive of the great nursing homes of the West End. I told Max what I had heard.

He picked up his office dictaphone without a word and dictated a memorandum to the Editor of the *Daily Express* which went something like this:

'I have just heard that So-and-So is out of a job, very ill, and in the London Clinic. I cannot imagine that in his present circumstances he can afford the fees of such a very expensive place. Will you therefore kindly go and see him, give him my warmest regards and good wishes, and tell him that he is not to worry, since we will meet the bill for all the fees. Meanwhile I hope he gets well.'

That was that.

When the Press Club was in a bad way financially, a year or two ago, he said that since the club frequently entertained all sorts of distinguished people to important functions they deserved a better dining-room. The old dining-room by that time was looking a bit part-worn. Max promptly donated £10,000. A top decorator was engaged and today the Press Club has a dining-room fit to stage its historic Derby luncheons, Justice Night, the annual Golf Night, the Children's Christmas Party which the Lord Mayor of London always attends and the many other functions which are attended by royalty, Cabinet Ministers, ambassadors and the like. So the Press Club which his father disapproved of (it was too near to the office and too easy for one to pop over for a quick double), has now got a new face-lift thanks to the generosity of his son. Moreover he and his wife are frequent guests of honour at Press Club functions, whereas Beaverbrook would never have set foot in the place.

Many memories of the human side of Lord Beaverbrook come back. I constantly received memoranda from him praising, criticising, or suggesting. His mind was always as active as a bee in a glass bottle. There was the morning when he received the weekly summary of advertising space in the London daily newspapers. One daily happened to be a few hundred column inches ahead of the *Daily Express* total for display advertising. He merely drew a ring round the two totals and wrote in his own hand at the bottom: 'sorrow, sorrow. B.' Other newspaper proprietors might have sent one a military or dictatorial rebuke.

Not so Beaverbrook. He knew that the soft word would be the sharpest spur to me.

He bought a large farming estate at Cricket St Thomas in the West Country, in which he took the greatest personal interest. Farming and the love of land was very near to his heart. One week-end on a long visit he persuaded, personally, a local dairy-man with a big distributive trade to buy the whole of the milk yield of the Beaverbrook herd. This little bit of off-the-cuff business, a mere flea-bite compared with his enormous newspaper and other financial turnovers, pleased him inordin-ately. He told me the whole story in all its detail with great pride in a memorandum and wound up by writing in his own hand: 'So you see, my dear Needham we are now both in the same business. I sell milk and you sell advertising.' He was as pleased as a schoolboy over the whole thing.

Beaverbrook had the old, traditional love of a good birthday party. He would organize them for other people. Other people, especially his own staff, would organize them for him. He loved to celebrate any triumph or occasion either glittering or homely with the enthusiastic invitation: 'Let's have a party!'

Therefore he was easy prey for a self-seeking exhibitionist like Hannen Swaffer. Swaff who liked sizzling in the limelight thought it was time he had a birthday party in honour of him-self. So he arranged one which was held in the Lincoln Room at the Savoy. About a hundred people, mostly from the worlds of journalism and literature, with one or two politicians and a smattering of the stage were invited. Swaff, having completed his list, crowned his planned self-glorification by inviting Lord Beaverbrook to take the chair. He agreed to do so. Beverly Baxter, then Editor proposed Swaffer's health with his usual oily flourish of saccharine compliments. Lord Beaverbrook spoke a few supporting words in which he paid a neat compliment to Swaffer's ability. Then he sat down.

The guests were preparing to get on with their dinner and their private chatter. This did not suit Swaff. He wanted the paean to peal forth unchecked. So he leant across to Beaverbrook and suggested that the latter should invite other guests to say a few words. Beaverbrook nodded and promptly called on this one and that one to get on their hind-legs and say a few kind words about that shrinking violet, Swaffer.

As far as I remember, at least four to six people spoke their little piece. The rest of us prayed that we might be allowed to get on with our dinner in peace. Not so Swaff. If his trumpeters had overblown themselves he still had enough wind to blow a final blast of self praise.

Casting a disapproving glance at the faces of his munching and guzzling guests he rose to his feet and tossing back his mane of white hair, struck a theatrical pose and stuttered, 'M-m-max and f-f-friends, I-I-I think that not enough has been s-s-said so f-f-far so I'm g-g-going to g-g-give you another s-s-speech.' And, damn his eyes, he did – with dreary repetition.

I often wondered who paid for that banquet.

Then, alas, on May 25th, 1964 came that tragic last party at the Dorchester when the great and the humble met for the last time to celebrate the 86th birthday of the man so many of us loved. It was the final heroic drop-curtain on the stage of a dramatic life which had galvanized this nation for more than half a century.

The party was inspired by Lord Thomson who owns *The Times, The Sunday Times* and a lot of other papers and magazines. He was a fellow-Canadian and comparatively new to Fleet Street.

In the past, we of the *Express* staffs had given 'the little man' more than one birthday party at the Dorchester. The last one, some years before, I remember well because, as a surprise, we had constructed on the ballroom floor a sizeable replica of the wooden, clapboarded manse in which his father, the Presbyterian minister, had lived with his family at Newcastle, New Brunswick in Beaverbrook's childhood. When the limelight went on, there was the wooden house, faithfully rebuilt in every detail. A small boy in a sailor suit came out on to the balcony and sang that popular sentimental ditty, 'Oh My Papa'. This was too much for Beaverbrook. His face suffused with emotion and the tears rolled down his cheeks as we all sang the chorus of the song. Later he thanked us for the party and said, 'No more parties. After all, who wants to celebrate a birthday when he is over eighty?'

Then, a few years later came the great Thomson party. The measure of Beaverbrook's fame and the affection in which so many held him can be gained from the list of some of the more notable people of all political parties and walks of life who were there. I remember seeing Viscount Rothermere, George Woodcock (Chairman – T.U.C.), Lord Normanbrook, the Earl of Longford, Lord Morrison of Lambeth, Lord Hill, William Deeds, M.P., Sir William Carr, Chairman of the *News of the World*, Sir Robert Fraser, Minister of Information, Sir Isaac Wolffson, the 'Gussies' stores millionaire, Lord Poole, Chairman of the Tory Party, Lord Devlin, Chairman of the Press Council, The Earl of Drogheda, Chairman of the *Financial Times*, the Rt. Hon. Iain Macleod, Lord Balfour of Inchrye, Hugh Cudlipp, Sir Patrick Hennessy, Chairman of the Ford Motor Company, Viscount Lambton, M.P., Paul Getty, reputedly the richest man in the world, Sir Alan Herbert, John Gordon.

Lord Thomson took immense pains to perfect every detail. It had meant endless correspondence and telephoning. He even flew a troop of the Royal North West Frontier Mounted Police over from Canada and what seemed like half a tribe of Red Indians in full war paint with eagles' feathers and full regalia.

During the afternoon I received a shock. Young Max said to me: 'You know Bill, my father is very ill indeed. I am not at all sure that he will be able to make it.'

I was horrified and said, 'Let us only pray that he can. We must have a wheel-chair ready at the door to take him to his place at the head of the table.

The chair was put there but never used.

Dead on time, Lord Beaverbrook arrived. Old, bent, infinitely frail with a parchment face, those bright eyes still glittered with intense fire. He recognized and knew everyone. He swept aside the proffered wheel-chair and, resting his right hand on the shoulder of his tall, stalwart son, he marched slowly through the guard of honour of the 'Mounties' in the vestibule, stiffly erect booted, spurred, breeched, their scarlet jackets a blaze of colour, revolvers on hip and hands gloved. The Red Indians, with their impassive faces, long black hair, ceremonial dress and feathered head-dresses made the perfect contrast to the rough-riding hard-boiled men from the North West Frontier. A roar of applause shook the ballroom and vestibule as 'the little man', obviously moved to the depths of his being, shuffled slowly into the full gaze of his standing, cheering guests. He walked the length of the room without faltering, took his seat at the head of the table and then gazed down the long dinner-jacketed ranks of the great and the famous who had come to pay him honour. It was the birthday party of the century.

After all speeches had been made, the compliments uttered, the good wishes waved to him, he was offered a sword. He took it in his right hand and solemnly cut his own birthday cake to a roar of cheers.

At the end he rose to his feet and, taking control of himself with obvious determination, he made the most impressive speech I had ever heard in my life. These words I shall remember for ever.

Reviewing his life, Lord Beaverbrook said, if my memory serves me right, 'All my life I have been an apprentice and never a master. I went into business as an apprentice but was never the master. I came over here and went into politics, again as an apprentice and was never the master. In journalism I began as an apprentice and was never the master [this was news to all of us!]. Now very soon I go some place else where I shall begin again as an apprentice but shall never be a master.' He died sixteen days later.

The Times, in its report of the dinner, quoted Lord Thomson who said:

" 'Lord Beaverbrook's career is truly an inspiration to every human being. Could anything better exemplify the limitless possibilities that lie before any poor boy anywhere?' Alluding to Lord Beaverbrook's activities as a politician as well as a newspaper owner, he added: 'We can never forget that he played a dominant and decisive part in the winning of the Second World War.'

"Trumpeters from the R.A.F. College at Cranwell – a reminder that Lord Beaverbrook was a major force behind the scenes in winning the Battle of Britain – played a fanfare as he entered the dining-room. Overhead were the flags of Canada, Britain, and the St Andrew's Cross of Scotland.

"Among other speakers was Lord Rothermere, who said: 'Lord Beaverbrook is unquestionably a most remarkable man in any kind of work. Whatever he would have taken up – whether in politics, newspapers or industry – he would have been bound to be a success.'

"Lord Beaverbrook, in reply, said: 'It is quite true that I am "old bones" but I still have something in the way of a head; I still have drive.'

"Reviewing his life in London he explained that he had sat for six or seven years in the House of Commons, saying very little, but possibly learning a great deal. 'I served Lloyd George,' he added; 'But it was very difficult to keep in step with that lively mind.'

"After his Parliamentary period came Fleet Street.

" 'I entered Fleet Street and became a slave of the Black Art, and did not know freedom for many years. I took over a bankrupt newspaper and lost a great deal of money. It was the fashion to have a Sunday paper, so I took over (actually he started it) the *Sunday Express* which added enormously to my losses but I did everything to make a good newspaper.

" 'The curious thing about journalism is that everyone knows more about it than the journalists themselves. There is an extraordinary opinion in the mind of mankind that each and every one of us could run a newspaper far better than the experts given the chance. I had the chance, but in learning about journalism I had to learn about journalists. No other profession is so heavily criticized and no other is told so frequently to mend its ways.

" 'I have a very simple code for us: do not ever print anything about anyone that you would not want people to read about yourself. The good journalist should write from his heart. He must be true to himself, he must have courage and initiative. He has no business to be despondent; he must be no respecter of persons and must be able to deal with all men from the highest to the lowest. We, as a nation, would be much poorer if the journalists were not there to protect us from hidden scandals and the misuse of power.'

"Turning to Lord Thomson, Lord Beaverbrook said he would suggest that for the future Lord Thomson 'should be guided by his wisdom and should begin again, get rid of his newspapers and take to politics or something'.

In a recorded tribute that night on the B.B.C.'s television programme, 'Panorama', the Duke of Windsor said: 'Lord Beaverbrook is a long-standing tried and trusted friend of the Duchess of Windsor and myself. He has had a full and successful life in the field of finance, politics, journalism and in the philanthropic scene.

'His name rides high in Canada, the land where he was born, and in Britain where he has mostly lived and worked, and throughout the British Commonwealth.'

A tribute from Sir Winston Churchill was included in a programme, 'Beaverbrook: the man and the myth,' on the B.B.C. Home Service. It was read by Lord Beaverbrook's son, Max Aitken:

'On my old friend's eighty-fifth birthday I recall the words I wrote of him in 1940: "Lord Beaverbrook rendered signal service. All his remarkable qualities fitted the need. His personal buoyancy and vigour were a tonic. I was glad to be able sometimes to lean on him. He did not fail; this was his hour. His personal force and genius, combined with so much persuasion and contrivance, swept aside many obstacles." '

Sir Winston's message went on: 'Time has but added to the intensity of what I then felt and to my regard and affection.'

Lord Beaverbrook's funeral less than three weeks after his moving speech was typical of the simplicity of the man. He was a devout Christian in the true sense of the word. He had an unshakeable simple faith in God and a withering contempt of the mumbo-jumbo panoply and formalism of organized churches which he considered obscured the simple truths and bare simplicity of Christ's message to mankind. This is made abundantly clear in a little book called *The Divine Propagandist* which he wrote. It was published by Heinemann in 1962 at 10s. 6d. two years' before the Beaver's death. I commend it to all who seek to find revealing light on the personality of that extraordinary man.

So, as you might expect, his funeral was utterly simple. It occupied just five lines of type in the *Daily Express* and other national newspapers. Just the bare announcement that his body had been cremated at Leatherhead on June 14th, 1964 and that the ashes had been taken to Cherkley. None but the family were present.

Later there was a memorial service at St Paul's Cathedral which was packed to the doors. Yet again the *Daily Express* and other newspapers published very brief accounts of the ceremony. Many hundreds of people, distinguished in the worlds of the Press, advertising, politics, finance, commerce and everyday life were there, but the only names mentioned were those of the Earl of Rosebery who gave a brief but very moving address – and was clearly moved himself as one could easily see – and Lady Beaverbrook, his son Max and Lord Denham who represented the Queen.

I thought as I came out of the cathedral, down the broad steps into the sharp light, in morning coat and silk hat, of the last funeral of a Press lord which I had attended. That was the funeral of the late J. S. Elias, the head of Odhams Press. He was a nice but undistinguished little man who began life as a printer, ended it as Lord Southwood and still remained a printer at heart and in outlook. He was given a magnificently impressive service in Westminster Abbey.

I was at my house on the Sussex coast for a few days. My secretary telephoned me to remind me of the service. I caught the train to London in a light holiday suit intending to hide myself away in the back seats of the Abbey. Unfortunately I was recognized by one of the ushers, who, despite my protests, lugged me off up the central aisle of the Abbey between packed rows of formally attired mourners, and, to my horror, dumped me in the middle of the choir stalls between Lord Rothermere, Lord Camrose and other Press lords all immaculately attired in morning dress. My holiday suit stood out like a bonfire. I would gladly have sunk through the floor into the peace of a vault.

CHAPTER NINE

Big Boys of Big Business

Advertising 'the Shop Window of the World' – Young Know-Alls
Who Know Little – How to Get Business – And the Cabman Who Was
Lost – How Sir Charles Higham Beat Sir William Crawford – George
Royds And His Glamour Girls – The Great Gordon Selfridge – His
Fantastic Rise and Fall – From Gold Plate and Royalty, Jewelled
Mistresses and Millions to a Pittance in Putney – 'I've Lived Too
Long'

My business in life is to get money – for other people. The
advertising world is the shop window of the world. We who
wheedle big sums out of big boys in big business in order to give
them nationwide displays of advertising matter are, let me whis-
per it, one of the mainstays of commerce. Without advertising
there would be no business and no prosperity. If you don't tell
the world about your goods they will never know of them and
therefore never buy them. All this is trite, but profoundly
true.

Therefore since advertising is the direct channel of communi-
cation between the maker, the seller and the buyer, it is, or
should be, an intensely personal and human affair. The man who
sells advertising space for a newspaper or any other media should
know his clients like brothers. He should be able to talk to them,
persuade them, laugh with them, condole with them in their
difficulties and, above all, help them with their selling problem.
All this can only be done by direct personal contact. That personal contact was, in my youth and until recent years, the main
principle on which one conducted business.

Today it seems to me that too many men in the advertising
business, particularly some of the bright young know-alls, have
not only lost the human touch. They never had it to begin with.
They lack the common touch which as Kipling rightly said is the
mark of a man who can mix with kings – and commoners.

Instead of this warm human contact between man and man,
too often they rely on statistics, market research – which has become one of the great ballyhoos – graphs and the dictaphone.
There is too much remote control – if control it is. Too many

people rely on the next man to see that the job is done and he in turn passes the buck to someone else, until the whole issue of getting the business is obscured and lost. Yet we poke fun at the Civil Servants in Whitehall, those past-masters at passing the buck.

Too many top men in the business of getting advertisements have never been out 'on the road' to get the business themselves. When I was young and in control of a large staff, I would not dream of asking any of our representatives to go out and do a job which I could not do myself.

There is an old saying in farming circles that 'the master's foot is the best dung on the land.' Equally, every good farmer prides himself that he can plough a straight furrow on his own land. Woe betide the ploughman who cannot equal the master's example. Equally, the advertisement manager should know the full technique of how to get advertisements by talking to, and persuading the client. He should come up the hard way if he is going to succeed in himself and bring revenue to his newspaper. Sending out glossy brochures, beautifully illustrated and gorgeously coloured, is no substitute for the handshake and the heart-to-heart talk on the spot.

Most of the bright young boys who draw up 'long term planning schemes' and design those gaudily glossy brochures don't know the first thing about the job of getting business. They sit importantly in their offices and expect it to come to them. How on earth, therefore, can they inspire the men on their staff to go out and do the job? How can they expect respect or stimulate initiative?

Let me, at the risk of seeming egotistical, give an example of what I mean. One morning at the daily conference of advertising staffs I said that a half page in the *Daily Express* in the next day or two would fall vacant and must be filled. That half would cost any advertiser who took it a cool £3,000 – when money was money and not an inflated symbol. I told my representatives that it was a test of initiative open to them all. The man who went out and got the job would have a feather in his cap, and I added, 'If I go out and get it myself you will know my reaction.' They looked at each other significantly. Then the conference was dismissed and one could hear their mutterings going down the corridor. The battle was on.

The next morning on my way to the office at 9 o'clock, I suddenly decided to call on a very important advertiser, whom I knew well, put the proposition to him and see what his reaction was. To my delight he said; 'Okay, we'll buy it.' The £3,000 half-page was in the bag.

Half an hour later one of my star representatives called on the same advertiser with the same proposition.

'I'm afraid you're too late,' he was told. 'Your governor was here half an hour ago and sold us the idea.'

The moral of this little story is that the man who was too late was never late again.

I am only too well aware of the danger of getting to know your customer *too* well, and becoming matey. Familiarity breeds contempt. On the other hand, if you do not know your man personally and have a shrewd idea of his strength and his weakness you cannot 'get under his skin' sufficiently well to sell him your ideas. It is all a matter of shrewd judgement of character and the use of psychology. It can also mean having to eat too many rich luncheons and swallow too many drinks. That is one of the hazards not only of advertising but of journalism itself. Both means high-pressure living, with mind and brain constantly alert.

It was not always so in the early days when I first entered Fleet Street. Until the outbreak of the 1914–19 war the frock-coat and top-hat were the uniform of the salesman and the hansom-cab or brougham was his means of getting about. The public house was too often his central venue. I recollect one very accomplished space-salesman, named Gill Godley, on a famous national newspaper who crowned a business deal with sheer music hall farce.

He took his client to a tip-top West End restaurant, dined and wined him extremely well, and by the time they got to the brandy and cigars, they were both almost under the table. The deal had been clinched.

To celebrate it, Gill suggested that they should toddle off to the Empire Theatre in Leicester Square and 'see the girls' on the famour Empire promenade. The Empire nightly attracted all the gay sparks in the West End. The client had no such yearning.

'Lesh go home, Gill, ol' boy,' he muttered thickly.

'Wh-whw-where do you live?' stuttered Gill, who was literally up to the gills.

'Cl-cll-Clapham, d-d-d-dear boy. W-w-w-ide and breezy. Losh of fresh air.'

'I l-l-live there too,' said Gill. 'Lesh get a hansom – and we'll have a d-d-drink on the way.'

They went out into the street, hailed a hansom-cab, climbed into it and told the driver their addresses in Clapham. As an afterthought, Gill Godley added, 'Lesh stop at every pub on the left-hand side of the road.'

The cabbie, in those days, sat high up in a little seat over and above the roof of the cab itself. There he was exposed to the wind and the rain.

Off they went. The cab stopped at every pub on the left-hand side. Each time, as they dismounted, Gill asked the cabbie to join them. The cabbie, like most of his kin, loved his drop of gin. He had a double at each pub. After the tenth or twelfth pub the cab-horse was trotting gently along under the gas lamps when Gill turned suddenly to his friend and said, 'Good God! We haven't stopped at the Horns at Kennington. It's the best pub on the road.'

At that moment a policeman stepped into the road, stopped the horse, took it by the bridle and said to the two in the cab, 'Gentlemen, where's your cab driver?'

Clearly, stunned by the gin, the cabbie had fallen off his box, and was lost somewhere in the dark wilderness behind them – clearly the other side of The Horns at Kennington. Luckily the horse knew the road by heart.

The big advertising agents of the Beaverbrook period were, and some still are, notable people by any standards of business. They deal in millions of pounds. They amass fortunes. Several have been rewarded with titles. Quite a few became national figures whose names were household words to the man in the street.

I think of Sir Charles Higham and Sir William Crawford as two men whose names constantly hit the headlines. Both were good public speakers and neither had any intention of hiding his light under a bushel. It always amused me at a public function where both men were due to speak to hear by office-telegraphy of the endless pains by which Charlie Higham, who was by far the better speaker of the two, almost always managed to get himself as the last speaker on the list. This gave him the chance to score off his old friend Sir William Crawford. Anyone who scored off Crawford deserved a medal.

Another great figure among advertising agents was the late Gordon Boggon, a kindly, likeable and eminently practical man of great vision who handled an enormous amount of business. Millions of pounds' worth of advertising passed through his hands. Others who have made their marks as personalities over the years include George Royds. There is a tale about him which is true. Up to the nineteen-twenties most of the big advertisers, that is the firms who spent their money lavishly on buying newspaper space, had their businesses in the North. Manchester was the capital of commerce. All the big woollen and textile businesses were in the North. The 'rag-trade' was largely centred up there at Leeds and elsewhere. Soap and cereals came mostly from the North, and bicycles from Birmingham and Coventry, and so one could go on with the list of everyday articles which needed advertising to sell them.

Then London and the South East of England began to expand as commercial and industrial centres. A shrewd man in Manchester, named Teddy Osborne of the Manchester firm of advertising agents, Osborne and Peacock, sensed the importance of the trend to the South. He realized that it had come to stay. Manchester would no longer be the centre of commercial gravity. So he searched round for a bright young man who was willing to go to London, set up an advertising agency and fight the battle of Fleet Street on its own doorstep. Very few young men did want to go to London. They did not want to risk leaving the headquarters.

One young man named George Royds had more courage and foresight. He volunteered for the job. He set up a London branch of Osborne and Peacock and went out and got business in a big way. I think his biggest fish in the net at that time and certainly the most glamorous from the public point of view was his capture of the advertising contract for Amami Shampoos. He coined the slogan 'Friday Night Is Amami Night'. That slogan with its photograph of pretty girls washing their hair went into every home in Britain.

Eventually he struck out on his own. Today the firm of G. S. Royds Ltd. is high up in the firmament of advertising agencies.

I have always believed, as I have said already, that any advertising manager worth his salt should keep in the closest and most human relationship with the big media executives of businesses which are likely to advertise through him. Always go for the man at the top. He is usually approachable. If you deal direct with him you cut out endless delays, and get quick decisions. Luckily, by pursuing these tactics throughout my business career I have been able to make many friends in big business who have remained friends, often long after they have retired from business.

Some years ago I had an idea, which I think was entirely original, of inviting fifteen or twenty prominent advertising agents and managing directors of big companies to dine with me at the Connaught Hotel, in a private room, and to bring with them their sons who had served in the Armed Forces. I invited only men whom I knew had sons who had fought for this country.

The result was that about thirty or forty fathers and sons turned up. After they had eaten a thoroughly well-chosen meal at which the chef had excelled himself, the port decanter began to circulate. It was then that I sprang my little psychological landmine.

'Gentlemen, I have invited you here tonight not only because you are all friends for whom I have great regard, but because every man among you has a son who has served in the Armed Forces in defence of this country. Most of you fathers did the same in the First World War, but tonight your sons are the guests of honour. I am going to ask each son round the table to say quite bluntly and truthfully if he thinks that this country was worth fighting for – now that he is back in it and looking, in many cases for a job, or shaping a career. You fathers will have to sit still and listen. We are the backroom boys tonight. Let the sons speak their minds. Gentlemen, pass the port.'

The effect on the company was amusing and a little surprising. Some of the fathers looked distinctly disconcerted. Practically all the sons perked up visibly. There were broad smiles from them and much nodding of heads. Clearly they were willing to speak their minds. However, the man sitting next to me looked down his nose and grunted: 'You won't get much out of my son. He can't put two words together. He doesn't even know how to speak.'

Later that father got the shock of his life.

I then invited each son in rotation to speak his mind. Naturally at this period of time I cannot remember what they all said.

Generally they were glad to be home, they did not for one moment regret having had to fight for Britain, but, like all Britishers, they were critical of the politicians and therefore critical in some degree of the set-up in the country. There were no embittered remarks and certainly no revolutionary or left-wing rubbish of the sort that we hear today from the half-witted young exponents of the 'permissive society'. One or two young men made speeches of outstanding clarity, sense and good oratory. I particularly remember Leonard Garland, son of the proprietor of Garland's Advertising Agency. He made a brilliant speech, but, then, he was always a master of words – and still is.

I remember him particularly because his father's career and mine had run very much on parallel lines in the early days. Sydney Garland was Advertisement Manager of the *Daily Mail* at the same time that I was Advertisement Manager of the *Evening News*. We had both been brought up under the Northcliffe umbrella. I think it's true to say that we were both appointed personally by Lord Northcliffe. Later Sydney struck out on his own and founded the highly efficient and prosperous business which bears his name today.

When they had all had their say came the surprise speech of the evening. The son of my next-door neighbour, the man who had grunted peevishly that his son could not put two words together, rose to his feet. He had a lot to say.

'I joined the Royal Air Force and the question that I have to answer is "have I come back to a world that I feel has been worth while fighting for?" I was glad to do my bit but the question is whether I thought it was worth while. That is the question of the Chairman who has asked me along tonight and I must say that I am not very enthusiastic.'

His father whispered to me, 'I told you he would be no good on his feet.'

The boy, the last speaker of the evening, went on to say: 'On my return I was bitterly disappointed by the decision of my father who was the boss of the Firestone Tyre Company in this country. He wanted me to go into the business. I am not in the least interested in motor-car tyres or any other rubber products. I was put on the road in a small car to travel as a rep. all over England and sell Firestone Tyres. I hated the job. So then my father suggested that I should be articled to a firm of solicitors. I am not interested in the law. But I saw quite clearly that my father had it at the back of his mind that if I became a lawyer I should be very handy as a ready-made adviser to keep him and his friends out of trouble.' The look on his father's face at that moment was unforgettable. The boy had hit him between wind and water. Then the boy went on: 'I don't care a damn about business, commerce, advertising, industry or the law. I know, somehow, that I have a use for my hands and perhaps a little touch of genius in my fingers. I want to be an artist.'

His father interjected: 'I told you so.'

The boy replied with spirit: 'An artist at least is a creator. A salesman is only a go-between. And a lawyer is a limb of the devil. I prefer to be an artist, if possible a creator of beauty. But my father will have none of it.'

The boy sat down defiantly, a little flushed. His father turned to me and said: 'You shouldn't have asked him to speak. He's a mixed-up kid.'

'Not a bit of it,' I said. 'The boy has spoken his mind. Now you know what he wants to do with his life. It's up to you to help.'

'How do I go about it?' the father asked.

'Send him to a good London art school, 'I said. 'Give him a chance to justify himself.'

Alfred (now Lord) Robens as President of the Advertising Association
presents the author with a glass beaker as 'Advertising Man of the Year'
in 1946

The author as 'Town Crier' at a Christmas Country Fair held at
Claridge's Hotel by the 'Thirty Club'

Master and Man: LWN with his boss, Sir Max Aitken (left)

'A waste of time,' the father objected.

In the end, reluctantly, he agreed to my suggestion and the boy was sent to an art school. He had not been there more than a few weeks before the most extraordinary thing happened. He was walking down a quiet, tree-shaded backstreet in Chelsea, one of those semi-village streets where the Londoner still finds old houses set in lovely gardens. Such a vision suddenly burst upon the boy's eyes. He came to a wrought-iron gate set in a high brick wall. It framed the vision of a lovely old English garden bright with flowers, shrined in green lawns with great trees over-arching. The centrepiece of this idyllic piece was an old red-brick Georgian house of grace. The perfect cameo of civilized English history.

The boy went home, got his paintbox, brushes, palette and easel and came back. he sat down at the gate and painted the picture in a sudden frenzy of admiration. He put his heart, his eyes and his paint-brush into that picture. He took it home and let it dry in his bedroom.

Next morning he took it to the school and showed it to his art master. The latter was most enthusiastic.

'This is a picture of uninhibited enthusiasm and beauty,' he said. 'You've really hit the high mark. It's so good that I am going to send it to the Academy and see if it has a chance of being hung. A chance in a thousand, but you never know, my boy. Meanwhile don't build your hopes too high. Wait and see. In any case, you've shown what you can do.'

He patted the young ex-airman on the shoulder, smiled benevolently and left the youngster in a tizzy of delight.

The miracle happened. The picture was accepted by the Royal Academy and was duly hung. On the opening day, the day of fashion and renown which in those post-war years marked the opening of the London 'season' itself, the Academy was, as usual, crowded with an elegant throng of top-hatted and tail-coated men, with their womenkind in the latest fashions. The young airman's picture was seen by a thousand sophisticated pairs of eyes. The great and the famous in Society, Art, business and commerce passed by it that day. Quite a few stopped to admire. No one, however, bought it. The little red tab which,

E

when stuck on the glass, means that a picture is sold was missing. For that matter it was missing from several hundred other pictures. Few artists expect to sell their first entry into the Academy on the first day. Many do not sell their pictures throughout the entire Academy season. They try to get a buyer afterwards.

I pointed out to the father that it was a great honour for his son to have hit the jackpot by having a picture accepted by the Academy at the first shot. He was not impressed. He said, rather ungraciously, that he still thought his son had picked the wrong vocation in life.

'But it's only a beginning,' I expostulated. 'It's a damn good beginning.'

'But he hasn't sold the picture yet,' the father objected.

'Neither have dozens of other artists,' I answered. 'Nobody except the top boys expect to sell a picture on the first day. Now if you want to encourage your boy who has obviously got great promise, the best thing for you to do is to go along to the Academy, find out what the reserve price is – it won't be much – and buy the picture. Tell them to keep your name secret. Your son is not to know that you have bought it. But there will be a red tab on it, he'll be as pleased as Punch and you will have given him a tremendous fillip in the career he has chosen for himself. He will then paint other pictures and better pictures, and probably before you know where you are, he'll be famous. And it won't cost you more than a few quid.' I still think that was sound advice.

Money meant nothing to that father. He had stacks of it. But he would not spend five, ten or even twenty pounds on buying his son's picture. He was determined not to encourage him as an artist. Personally I was terribly disappointed. The father went down in my estimation a lot.

The sequel is not dramatic, but it has perhaps a touch of pathos. The father is dead. The son, so far as I know, has never had another picture accepted by the Royal Academy. One does not hear his name mentioned as an artist. He earns his living, I believe, as a commercial artist doing a more or less routine job, drawing pictures, designs and the like to order. No doubt his father would say, if he were alive, that his son is a business failure. I feel convinced that the young man, if he has not found fame, has at least found happiness. He is doing what he wants to do, expressing himself in his own way, and although he may not earn the tens of thousands of pounds which his father put in the bank he is at least happy in his soul. Surely that is the secret of making the most of this life.

Talking of big men in the advertising world, which is the world also of super-salesmen, I consider that the late Gordon Selfridge, founder of the monumental store in Oxford Street which bears his name, was the greatest salesman of my time, or, if you like, of this century.

Harry Gordon Selfridge was born in a small town called Ripon in Wisconsin which made him an American citizen. He was brought up at another small unknown town called Jackson, in Michigan, which is now better known because pop-singers constantly put it into their hyena lyrics.

Mr Selfridge as a boy was fascinated by the heroes of history. He read avidly of the deeds of Charlemagne, Marco Polo, the Great Mogul and Constantine. They were great warriors, explorers and conquerors. Mr Selfridge determined to be a bit of them all. He also read the gilded stories of the great merchants of Genoa, Venice and Florence and was enthralled not only by their riches and luxury but by their palaces, their dinner services of gold and silver plate, their jewels and their troops of slaves. Out of all this reading he built up for himself a picture of what he used to call 'the romance of commerce'. He wrote a very readable book on that subject. So you may say that, as a boy, he made up his mind to become a merchant prince, and this he did. He started off as an apprentice with the great trading house of Marshall Field and Company in Chicago, became a partner and then fixed his eyes on London.

He came to London with plenty of money in his pocket, a head full of revolutionary ideas and set up not a shop but a great store. Now the great store was a new thing in the shopping world of those pre-1914 days. Londoners were accustomed to buy their goods from small individual shops. The better quality the goods the more exclusive and family-like was the shop. Many

London shops had descended from father to son for generations. Their customers, equally, had patronized them for as many generations. It was unthinkable that any outsider, particularly an American, could 'bust open' the long-established English practice and tradition of buying clothes, boots, guns, food, cigars, linen or even matches and candles from any shop other than the high-class family business in the West End or 'the little shop on the corner'. Selfridge set out to conquer both those worlds. Largely he succeeded. The end-product was, and is, a vast store of many floors which caters for almost every degree of taste and purse.

Selfridge himself lived in incredible luxury. He rented one of the greatest town houses of London in the days when dukes and earls had London houses which were virtually palaces. There he entertained the highest in the land – and they dined off gold and silver plate. He had a great steam-yacht called *Conquerer* – the sort of name he would choose – in which he and his guests went on world cruises. He had two highly decorative, highly jewelled Hungarian mistresses known as The Dolly Sisters who were as famous on the stage as they were for their association with him. He was reputed to have spent a huge fortune on them. He showered them with jewels, money, furs, motor-cars and world luxury tours. Many years later, when he was in sad financial straits, and was old and white-haired, I saw him standing in the queue for the five-and-ninepenny seats at a cinema waiting to see a film in which the Dolly Sisters starred.

In spite of his extravagance, luxury and opulence which made him internationally famous, Selfridge was none the less a shrewd operator in business and a down-to-earth salesman.

I first came in contact with him soon after his big store had got into its stride. He was making advertising news by buying page after page of advertising space in the great newspapers. This cost him hundreds of thousands of pounds. It was a novel thing to do. Up to that time the London stores had never taken more than a few square inches of crowded print in which to tell the reader what they had to sell.

Selfridge's full-page advertisements hit the newspaper reader like bludgeons. They did not advertise one single item of goods for sale. Instead they proclaimed the name of Selfridge in tremendous type, highly decorative. Underneath that were knights in armour, charging into battle on splendid steeds with lances couched and pennons flickering.

Other pages showed merchant princes of medieval times sailing the purple seas in their great carracks and caravels, loaded presumably with the riches of Genoa, Venice and Naples. There were other equally arresting and challenging figures. All of them, I have no doubt, sprang from the youthful reading away back in Jackson, Michigan of the young American boy who had found inspiration in the doings of Charlemagne and Constantine, in the travels of Marco Polo and the splendid voyages of that great merchant prince, Cosimo Medici. Thus were childish dreams realized in full splendour by a middle-aged man with a ruddy face, a boyish smile, a brisk manner and a genius for making friends and summing-up enemies.

The extraordinary thing about Selfridge's store was that when you, as the customer, walked into it, nobody tried to sell you a thing. There were no shop-walkers in frock coats and striped trousers to greet you with a decorous bow as was the custom in any good-class London shop. You just wandered around to look, to appraise and to buy if you felt like it.

You, as a customer, would be cheered on your way by notices displayed prominently in every department on every floor. In bold type they proclaimed: THE CUSTOMER IS ALWAYS RIGHT. Selfridge himself coined this phrase. It was, without exaggeration, revolutionary. It put the rest of the shopkeepers back on their haunches. They were made to feel that they were on the defensive. The implication was that their service was wrong. The same slogan appeared in every newspaper in which Selfridge advertised. The result was that the customers flocked to the great gilded wrought-iron doors of the new store in Oxford Street. It *must* be right to shop there because you, as the customer, were, according to Mr Selfridge, always right. That slogan probably coined millions for Selfridge.

Now Mr Selfridge himself might have been giving a great dinner, eaten off gold plate, with powdered flunkeys in attendance the night before and the guests at his London palace might have been dukes, earls, ambassadors, field marshals, and millionaires, but if you walked into Selfridge's store at nine o'clock next morning you would be sure to see a brisk, dapper man with a ruddy face and a trimmed moustache, a silk hat on his head, walking from department to department, speaking to this one and that one, with a nod or a wave to the humblest employees. That was Gordon Selfridge on the job.

You, a shopper, might have come up from Balham or have just walked across the road from Berkeley Square. Mr Selfridge would fix his eye on you, advance with brisk dignity, raise his silk hat, and ask you politely if you were satisfied with 'the store' and if it provided everything and anything which you wanted. If there were any faults and omissions he would be delighted to hear of them. That was the super-salesman of the shop floor.

I personally found that he was a super-salesman in quite another way. I rather prided myself that after long training and with, I hope a certain gift of the gab, plus a very real enthusiasm for the selling powers of my own newspaper, that I could persuade the most hard-headed business man to take space in the *Daily Express*. Usually it came off. Not so with Gordon Selfridge. He knew precisely what he wanted and he was not going to spend a penny more on another square inch of space.

I remember particularly one day when we had a very attractive proposition to put to him. I was in full swing, explaining precisely why the paper, on a special day, would have an extra-special national appeal and it would be worth his while to take at least another page of advertising. I expatiated with enthusiasm, with facts, and at length. I was half-way through my paean when Mr Selfridge suddenly leant across his great desk, and with a charming smile said gently, 'Tell me, my dear Needham, have you been to Germany lately? What was it like? I rather think I'd like to take a trip up the Rhine and see the vineyards. Do tell me where, and when, to go.'

That shut me up. He employed the same tactics with other salesmen. He could cut down the fine flower of oratory with one deft swipe. I retreated baffled.

A few days later I turned up again with E. J. Robertson, the General Manager, as hard-headed a business man as Selfridge, to try and finalize the contract. I thought the pair of us might just about be a match for him. Not a bit of it. Mr Selfridge listened politely to most of what we had to say. Then when he had had enough of it, he suddenly switched to Robertson, subjected him to a lively cross-examination on the subject of Germany. And insisted that the *Daily Express* ought to send me out there.

This was simply skilful side-tracking. There was no reason why any of us should go to Germany. Mr Selfridge slipped it in as the spanner which wrecked our works. Such was his charm of manner no one could possibly be offended.

Gordon Selfridge was famous, firstly for his daily luncheons to which he invited people of note, but more especially for his Election Night parties to which he invited five hundred of, presumably, the most famous people in Britain to a splendid jamboree in the roof garden at Selfridge's with champagne, illuminations, caviare, cold salmon – and election results. To be invited was a hallmark. I was fortunate enough to be invited a good many times.

In those days, in the Roaring Twenties, these parties were the talk of London. The guests varied from people such as the Prime Minister or Winston Churchill to Beaverbrook or the Dolly Sisters. Since then the idea has been taken up and copied (without acknowledgements) by many other stores, by newspapers and by private people who wish to capture a brief moment of publicity.

It seemed in those gay, extravagant, days and starlit nights that the ship of Selfridge could never founder. Like his great yacht *Conqueror*, his store was also the conqueror of shop-keeping in London. He himself was the epitome of personal success. The thought of financial failure was ridiculous. One took it for granted that uncounted millions ballasted the ship of Selfridge. This modern merchant prince seemed as rich as Croesus.

Then came the shock. The power and prestige of store and man alike began to decline. There were whispers of financial fractures. Doom seemed to be overtaking the Selfridge empire. Now as I understand it – and I have not yet seen it printed any-where else – the cause of the decline and fall of Gordon Selfridge was a deal which he concluded with an old-fashioned but very hard-headed Scots shopkeeper named Laurie. Mr Laurie was the power behind Whiteley's, the great store in Westbourne Grove which, for many years, had been the shopping centre of the well-to-do families of Bayswater just as Harrods was the 'big shop' for the residents of Kensington and Knightsbridge. Neither of them held the unique position of Selfridge's.

Now I have good reason to understand that Mr Laurie drove a hard bargain so shrewdly that even that shrewd operator, Harry Gordon Selfridge, the old fox of shopkeeping, was out-foxed himself. Selfridge's was put, more or less, in pawn.

The decline and fall of Mr Selfridge was almost as rapid and certainly as decisive as his rise to fame in London in the years just before the First World War. He was politely retired from the board of Selfridge's, the control of which was taken over by a large financial interest. His London palace was given up. He spent his last years in a small flat on Putney Hill with his daughter who had married a penurious foreign prince whose name I forget. In her father's heyday her princely title figured largely on his guest lists.

Now an extraordinary thing happened to me years after the poor old gentleman had ceased to hit the headlines. I was passing by the front door of his great store from control of which he had been ousted years before, when I walked slap into him on the pavement. He was looking spruce and erect as usual although he was well past ninety. He shook hands warmly. He greeted me with all his former boyish enthusiasm. We talked for a few moments of the great days, his days of glory and splendour. Then he looked at me with a sudden sadness, dropped his voice and said, 'I've lived too long, Needham' I made the proper sympathetic sounds. We shook hands and parted again. He went home and died that night.

This story, oddly enough, is told in that very good biography of Selfridge which was written by that capable journalist, Reginald Pound. Reggie Pound is a first-class biographer, as is proved by his life of Northcliffe, written in collaboration with Sir Geoffrey Harmsworth.

There had been a previous book about Selfridge, written by

one Billy Williams, one-time Advertising Manager of Selfridge's. He and I had done a lot of business together over the years. He left Selfridge's on a pension some time before Mr Selfridge himself was retired from the boards.

Billy Williams proceeded to show his gratitude towards the employer who had given him a good job and high pay by writing a tasteless book about Selfridge. He had no literary style or ability but he apparently thought that he could offset this and make the book into a best seller by re-quoting all the outworn gossip and scandal about the Dolly Sisters and other aspects of "the old man's" life. It all seemed rather unnecessary since whatever Selfridges' minor human faults might have been – and most of us have them – he was a great man by any standards. Reginald Pound's book however, put the story of this remarkable man in its true perspective. He was commissioned by the board of Selfridge's to write an honest biography of the founder because they were, not unnaturally, displeased by the muck-raking of the amateurish literary aspirant, Mr Williams.

The sardonic aspect of this remarkable personal epic is the fact that whereas Selfridge, in his zeal to revolutionize London's shopping and to put the old-fashioned shop-keeper out of business was, in the long run, beaten at his own game by an old-fashioned shopkeeper, Mr Laurie, whose name is virtually unknown to the world which once knew Selfridge as a headline in every newspaper.

CHAPTER TEN

Ad-Men and Odd Men

When Barmaids Bolt – I Steal the Chief Constable's Motor-Car –
Three Pretty Girls Have the Last Laugh – Big Money at Cards – I
'Hold Up' a Bank – And Get Away with Thousands – The Fantastic
Major Buckley – 'I've Cleaned up a Tidy Handful' – And so to Major
General – Taking the Gate-Money in Heaven

The good advertising salesman must have the nose of a fox-
hound, the cunning of a fox, the hide of a rhinoceros, the suction-
capacity of a hippo, the genial grin of a bull-dog and the
stamina of all these animals put together.

Therefore, when a bunch of what are known as 'ad-men'
are together, the heavens weep, barmaids run for shelter, head
waiters hold out their hands, and the town chosen for their
annual debut, felicitously known as a convention, is lit with a
reddish glow after dark. As a breed they are a jolly lot.

They will be as sincere as a Methodist preacher during their
business discussions, as Wise as Diogenes, but the moment business is over, the schoolboy in each man is let out. God help the
man who cannot hold his liquor or keep his head. They work
hard in the face of rebuffs, disappointments and defeats but they
never give in, and when the day's work is over they play hard. I
have attended advertising conventions over many years at such
resort towns as Brighton, Torquay, Eastbourne, Harrogate,
Newcastle and in Scotland.

There was one epic night in the Grand Hotel at Harrogate
when, after a splendid full-dress dinner, we all sat down in white
ties and tail-coats to play poker, until dawn came shy-footed
over the Yorkshire moors. The party consisted of what one
might call the élite of the advertising world, men who talked and
dealt in millions and counted their incomes in thousands. Young
Needham, full of bounce and eagerness, was delighted to be of
the party.

When the first pallid light lit the streets outside it dawned
upon some of us that we were a mile or so from our own hotel,
that not a taxi was to be had for love or money and that a dawn

stroll in full evening dress through the ultra-respectable streets of Harrogate might make the sparrows laugh. A large, long, low red motor-car stood on the gravel outside the hotel windows. It offered the immediate solution. How to start it was the problem. We borrowed a hairpin from a lion-hearted chambermaid, and one of the party who had a rudiment of engineering knowledge – or may have been a part-time burglar – probed about in the inner mysteries of the motor-car until it started. The rest was easy. We were at our hotel within minutes and left this conspicuous motor-car parked decorously to one side of the front door.

A hot bath, a change of clothes, a good breakfast and we were out on the golf course without a wink of sleep. The sharp Yorkshire air and the exercise worked wonders.

That evening we changed into white tie and tails once more, piled into one or two taxis and arrived, spruce and fit, for another function at the Grand Hotel. I was stopped in the hall by the hall porter who said with a lowering frown, 'I believe you gentlemen drove away a large red motor-car from this hotel this morning. It's a serious matter because it amounts to theft and, whats' more, it belongs to one of the most important people in all Yorkshire. Have you got that motor-car, sir?'

'Got it? Good heavens, no. We went back in a grey Wolseley. I remember it only too well because it was barely big enough to hold the lot of us. But,' I paused and pondered for a moment, 'now you mention it, I *did* notice a red motor-car outside the hotel entrance as we came away this evening. It caught my eye because it's a long low car, and I thought to myself that it could probably knock up a pretty hot mileage.'

The hall porter regarded me disbelievingly. 'Just one moment, sir. Kindly wait there until I telephone.' He did so. Our hotel informed him that the red motor-car was still outside. Moreover, they said, quite truthfully, that they had not seen anybody drive it there. The hall porter's face cleared a little. He came back to me and, with the air of a magistrate presiding over a juvenile court said, 'You're lucky, sir. The car's there. I'll say no more about it, but you might as well know that it belongs to the Chief Constable of the West Riding of Yorkshire.'

Now the man who started the motor-car with such burglarious skill was a very good friend of mine, George Burnside, an advertising agent of high repute. He and I and another man got ourselves involved in another somewhat juvenile farce at another convention held in Newcastle-on-Tyne. The organizers invited half the pretty girls in Newcastle to come along and act as dance partners to 'tired business men'. Full of Christian charity they jumped at the chance. The hotel was flooded with pretty shop-girls and other beauties.

We three took a passing fancy to our three lady partners and at the end of the evening – early in the morning – very properly and gallantly offered to drive them home. We climbed into three separate taxi-cabs, not knowing that the three girls all lived at the same address some miles out of Newcastle. When we arrived there full of hope and joy we handed out our lady friends, paid off the cabs and dismissed them, hoping that we might be invited into the house for another little party. Not a bit of it. The ladies had decided that the tired business men had better go home to bed. They slammed the door in our faces.

So, we were left to face the dreary prospect of trudging at least five miles in the grey dawn, through grey suburban streets into the heart of Newcastle, in full evening dress without a clue as to the proper direction. We walked for miles. George Burnside who had a good heart but was no athlete was further handicapped by the fact that he had tight evening shoes. A dormant corn sprang into malevolent life when he had covered the first three or four miles. He subsided with a groan of agony on to the kerb and said in piteous tone, 'Bill, I'm done for. My feet are killing me. There's a telephone box over there. For God's sake ring the hotel and tell them to send a car. We must have a couple of miles to go yet, and I just can't do it.'

I rang the hotel. They promised to send a car. I told them precisely where we were since I had noticed the name of the street. I went back to poor George and comforted him.

'We'll probably have to wait half an hour, old boy, before the cab turns up. Have a cigarette and cheer up.'

'I don't smoke,' said he morosely, nursing his corn.

'God, I could do with a bath right now.'

The next moment a car rounded the corner, pulled up and a uniformed driver opened the door for us. We told him the address of the hotel. He made no comment. Two minutes' later he deposited us at the front door of the hotel. We had walked the whole five miles and were only just round the corner when George's corn went on strike.

George was the centre-piece in another little near-farce. One of the hazards or penalties of a responsible job in the advertisement world is that, in the sacred cause of getting business, one must be prepared not only sometimes to eat too much, to drink to an heroic limit, but also to be able to sit down and play a hand at cards against men who are prepared to bid in hundreds. This is where the sensible 'ad-man' must keep his head. He cannot charge his gambling losses to office expenses although he can charge an expensive luncheon or dinner party with perfect justice.

George was playing 'Slippery Sam' one night at the advertising convention in Harrogate. One of his opponents was Ted Osborne, chief of the well-known advertising agents, Osborne and Peacock. He was a strong personality, a bit of a rough diamond with a brusque manner and a kind heart under it all. George lost a good deal of money to him.

The game had gone on until dawn and as time progressed it got out of hand. A lot of ready money had been put into the pool. Finally most of the players ran out of ready cash. George was among them. Those who knew him realized, firstly, that such a substantial loss could hit his private bank balance rather too hard and, secondly, we knew only too well that he had far too much pride to complain, to make excuses or wriggle out. He was not that sort of man. When he totted up his losses he turned to Ted Osborne and said, 'I haven't got that sort of money on me. I'll have to write out a cheque.'

He wrote a cheque for the amount, signed it George Sprakely Burnside and handed it across the table to Ted Osborne. Now Ted, like the rest of us, only knew him as George Burnside. We knew nothing of his unusual middle name. Ted saw that this gave him a loop-hole to enable him to cancel George's debt without allowing the latter to feel in any way humiliated or under an obligation to him. He glared at the cheque, looked up and growled, 'This won't do. I can't put that in the bank. It's not your name.'

'But I sign all my cheques that way,' George expostulated. 'Sprakely is my second Christian name. If I signed it any other way the bank wouldn't pass it.'

'You're George Burnside to me,' Ted retorted, 'and you're George Burnside to all the rest of us. I don't recognize this signature and what's more I'm damn well not accepting this cheque with a name on it that means nothing to me.' Thereupon he tore the cheque up.

It was no use George Burnside protesting that the cheque was perfectly all right and would go through the bank. He started to write another one. Ted Osborne brushed it aside and said brusquely, 'The whole thing's off. This name on this cheque is no bloody good to me – so the whole thing's off.'

Thus, the tough old Northerner with a kindly glint in his eye saved George a pain in his bank balance and, at the same time, saved his pride. Ted could well afford to lose the money but he knew well enough that George could not.

Poor old George, alas, died years later when he had climbed the ladder of success to become Chairman of Irwin, Wasey, the important American advertising agency. He and his wife went out to do their Christmas shopping and returned home after a long slogging, jostling tour of the shops. George complained of being tired and said that he was going into the bedroom to lie down and have a little rest.

'All right, darling,' said his wife, 'I'll roast some chestnuts for you at the sitting-room fire and call you when they are ready. You always love them.'

A few minutes later, when the chestnuts were popping in their brass roaster, she went into the bedroom. George was dead.

Once again I had to face the sad duty, which has been my part too often, of paying a final tribute, in the form of an address, at the memorial service to my old friend which was held in a large, fashionable church at the back of the Albert Hall. So passed a man of sterling worth and great ability. It ended a friendship which had warmed my life for many years.

I have referred to the health hazards of having to eat too many rich meals, drink too many drinks and sit up playing cards into far too many dawns which are part of the advertising business. Mind you, I am a person of simple tastes. I ask little of this life other than the first oyster of the season, the first grouse of the season, the first partridge in September and the best vintage year of Krug champagne – simple but laudable tastes which somehow always taste much better when the luncheon or dinner is crowned by the fact that one secures another full page of advertising at the top rates.

Many a big deal has been concluded over such a menu. It is fun while it lasts but if that sort of thing lasts too long, retribution is round the corner. No man of sense will eat or drink too much unless he counter-balances it with hard exercise. The golf course has been my salvation, and, for that matter, army training was the rock on which my constitution was founded. Young men who have never had army training do not know what a valuable legacy they have missed.

Oddly enough I was fortunate enough to pull off one of the most successful coups of my career, and one which made business history, over two cups of tea.

Not many years ago 'the young master', otherwise Sir Max Aitken, asked me in the course of a personal talk, 'Bill, why don't the banks advertise with us? They've got millions of money and they spend very little on advertising. Apart from a few inches of small type reporting the chairman's speech at the Annual General Meeting what does the average bank spend with the newspapers? Damn all! Go out and get. If anyone can do it, you can, Bill.'

This was a direct challenge. It was the sort of challenge that Beaverbrook would have thrown down like a gauntlet. I accepted it.

I went back to my office, picked up the telephone and rang up the General Manager of Lloyd's Bank at their head office in the City of London. The *Daily Express* banked with them. Therefore they were my obvious target.

I said to the General Manager's secretary, 'My name is Needham. I am a Director of Beaverbrook Newspapers, I would very much like to have a few moments to talk business with the General Manager at his convenience.'

There was a moment's pause at the other end whilst the message was conveyed to the General Manager. He, I do not doubt, jumped to the conclusion that Beaverbrook Newspapers were on the verge of some great financial development in which the bank would play it's part. Big business was obviously on the way. He invited me cordially to come round to his office at once.

I arrived at the head office within minutes. The reception was quite staggering. A uniformed commissionaire directed my motor-car to a private parking-place. I was bowed into the bank, escorted through endless corridors and ushered finally into a palatial office where sat the General Manager. He offered me a cup of tea.

Over the Earl Grey's Mixture I came straight to the point. I told him that although banks gave the public a tremendous and varied service they never advertised the fact. It was high time that Lloyd's Bank paved the way. And I went on, a full page advertisement in the *Daily Express* would reach several million readers and would cost them no more than around £5,000. It was, I said, an obvious investment with a tremendous potential yield.

His face fell. The vision of fresh millions being poured into the Beaverbrook account faded. I was not bringing *him* money. I wanted *his*. He pondered the matter. It was a revolutionary suggestion. No bank up to that time had even dreamt of taking a full-page advertisement in the popular Press. One probably felt that they regarded it as infra dig.

The manager, after a moment's thought, said:

'This, of course, would be an entirely new departure. It is something so completely out of tradition that I cannot give a decision myself. I shall have to consult my colleagues on the board. Mr Needham, I will put the proposition to them, and I will get in touch with you again in a few days time. Do have another cup of tea.'

I went back to my office in a state of hope, excitement and apprehension. If I pulled it off it was not only the answer to Max Aitken's challenge and the complete justification of his foresight but it would be an historical landmark in the history of advertising itself. It seemed almost too much to hope for. One envisaged the bank Directors solemnly shaking their heads and saying that anything so vulgar, so ostentatious and so 'unprofessional' as a full-page advertisement in the *Daily Express* was quite unthinkable. It would lower the dignity of the bank. It might even make them a laughing-stock in the City. These thoughts haunted my slumbers for a night or two.

Then came a telephone call from the bank. The General Manager would be delighted to see me. Once again the cup of fragrant China tea. This, I thought is the good old turn-down. The polite way of saying 'no'.

'Mr Needham,' he said, 'we have decided to accept your proposition. The bank will take a full-page advertisement in the *Daily Express* on the terms you have put to us. Do have another cup of tea.'

That 'hold-up' was, I like to think, in its little way, a landmark in advertising and banking history alike. Since that day every other big bank has followed suit. Today bank advertisements vie with each other to catch the customers. Their advertising appeals vary in language from the stately to the coy. Some are even positively skittish.

Very different was the saga of Major Buckley. He was one of the most extraordinary characters I have met. It all began when I went to the City offices of a small old-fashioned firm which made and exported tinned foods. Their main customers, believe it or not, were missionary societies on the West Coast of Africa. As the missionary business was then past its peak of Victorian enthusiasm for converting the black man, business was beginning to drop off. The members of the board struck me as being honest and amiable greybeards who were a little bewildered by the gradual deterioration of their long-established customers.

In an outer office I ran into a big, bluff military-looking man with a forthright manner. He oozed self-confidence. He introduced himself on the spot, announced that he was Major Buckley, late of the Indian Army and added that he had spent a short time in America studying public relations which he had found 'damned amusing' and that he had been called in by the tinned-food firm to advise them on how to solve the problem of their declining business. He added handsomely that he was a complete amateur at the job. Whilst he was talking, his secretary was packing up his papers and emptying his desk.

'I've handed in my report, Needham,' he told me. 'And now we're packing up. I'm off to the next job if I can find one. I'm just going to pop in to say goodbye to the old gentlemen in the board room and then we'll call it a day.'

He went into the board room. I decided to wait for him. A quarter of an hour later he came out beaming.

'Unpack my papers. Put everything back in the desk,' he said to his secretary. 'They like my ideas so much they've made me Managing Director.'

A few days later he got in touch with me, announced that he was starting an advertising campaign, proposed to engage advertising agents and would like to have my advice and suggestions. Would I like to have luncheon with him? I did so, at the inevitable Savoy Grill. I gave him as much good advice as I could think of, and eventually collected a little advertising from his company. Then I lost sight of him again. One assumed that his company was staggering along, bravely fighting its last-ditch battles.

Then again I ran into Major Buckley in my happy hunting ground, the Savoy Grill. He was sitting at a table, larger than life, demolishing a good luncheon and asked me to join him. He called for a bottle of champagne instantly. At that moment it flashed through my mind that here was another version, in living form, of the one and only Valentine Castlerosse. Like Castlerosse he was larger than life and he obviously enjoyed work as much as he enjoyed play.

'How's the firm going?' I asked.

'Splendidly,' he said. 'It's gone! I've just sold it out to Beecham's at a hell of a good price and all the old boys are happy. So am I. I've cleaned up a tidy little handful.'

Once again the curtain fell on the ebullient, unquenchable Major Buckley. I lost touch with him for a year or more. Then I had to go over to New York on business. I had not been in my hotel more than twenty-four hours before the telephone rang.

'A gentleman named Major Buckley wishes to speak to you, sir.'
A moment later he was on the line. He had spotted my name
among the list of arrivals by ship from England. We met for a
noggin in the hotel bar. I asked him what he was doing in
America.

'I'm here on behalf of Beecham's to tidy up their interests in
North and South America,' he said. 'I've been up to Canada and
had a look round there. I've had to get rid of certain executives
and tighten up the organization generally. I'm off to South
America within a few days to do the same thing.'

Once again Major Buckley disappeared from my ken. Then,
months later, back in London, I had lunch with my friend Lazell,
the Chairman of Beecham's. I asked for news of Major Buckley.
He roared with laughter.

'The major is no longer with us. I'm bound to say I always
admired his dashing cavalier way of dealing with things, but I
came to the conclusion that unless I got rid of him he would very
soon get rid of me!'

That, I thought, was the end of Major Buckley. Not a bit of
it. Years later, when the Second World War broke out, part of
my wartime stint was to organize the collection and salvage of
waste paper, millions of tons of which were badly needed. The
War Office, in the opinion of most newspapers, was one of the
principal wasters of paper. So off I went to the military holy of
holies to find out who was the man responsible for salvage.

I was ushered into a large room at the end of a stone-paved
corridor with the words: 'The general will see you, sir.' There
sitting at an enormous desk, gorgeously apparelled in the uniform of a major-general, red tabs and all, sat my old friend
Buckley.

'Good God, Bill, what on earth are you doing here?' he said
explosively. 'I might as well ask what the hell you're doing,
done up in all your glory as a major-general,' I said laughingly.

He rose to his feet, large, fat and jolly, beaming with optimism
and success, shook me warmly by the hand and said, 'I was
brought in to stop these War House chaps wasting so much
money. Like you, I'm part of the economy drive.'

'But why on earth did they make you a major-general?' I
persisted.

'Because I've saved the country millions of pounds,' he said quite seriously. 'Among other things I've persuaded the War Office to do away with the Sam Browne equipment. The belt and shoulder strap, which used up so much leather, took so much time to polish and was completely out of date as far as modern war is concerned, have gone. It was an anachronism. I have persuaded them to adopt the built-in webbing belt as part of the tunic.' And he added, laughing, 'you, as an old soldier, will know that to get the War House to agree to such a change as that is like winning a battle in itself.'

I left the general effulgent in his glory, having won another of his battles with life. There was something peculiarly British about that man. He was the eternal bobbish schoolboy. He was the sort of chap who would have come out on top of any situation anywhere. For the rest of the War I heard and saw no more of him.

When peace came I was invited to the centenary celebrations of Harrods by my friend Sir Richard Burbidge, the Managing Director, who incidentally served in my division in the First War. A great many distinguished people were there. And who, among the most distinguished, should be there but – Major-General Buckley! He was in civilian dress but one felt that at any moment he might take over Harrods or go out and win the next World War. When the party was over and the guests had gone, inevitably Burbidge, Buckley and Needham gravitated by homing instinct to the Savoy Grill where we dined until long past midnight.

Since then our paths have not crossed. But I hear that the unquenchable Buckley is one of the best bridge players in London, a shining light of the Portland Club and as rumbustious as ever. He will, if I know him, still be gay, gallant, invincible and invariably accompanied by a beautiful lady. 'None but the brave deserves the fair,' but somehow the Buckleys get the most beautiful.

If I do not run into my old friend again, I feel sure that if, and when I ascend to Heaven, there will be Major-General Buckley sitting at the golden gates – taking the entrance money!

CHAPTER ELEVEN

Showering Money

How a Vast Fortune Was Made – The Baby Deer Which Is God's Gift to Little Girls – A Rolls-Royce as 'a Little Present' – New York Interlude – 'Throw Those Blondes Out' – Miss Dixie Tighe Takes Over – A Woman Of Steel – The Vinous and Invincible Mr Gooding – I 'Insult' the Lord Mayor Of London

One of the most fascinating, and light-hearted stories of a monumental advertising success of the present day is that of the well-known drink, Babycham, which put its manufacturers on the road to fortune and many a pretty little girl on top of her dancing form, gay but clear-headed.

It came about in this way. Down in the West Country, in a sleepy old Somerset town, dozing among the apple and pear orchards, was an old-fashioned, steady-going family firm, called Showering and Sons. It might just as well have been called Showering and Grandsons, for true to the paternal tradition of rural England, the board included grandfathers, fathers and grandsons. It was 'family' in the best and truest sense. It did a steady trade in its own area, but by no stretch of the imagination could it be called a firm of national importance, or nationwide sales. It just jogged along, comfortably prosperous – but over-loaded, during one particular season, with a vast amount of perry. Perry is the cider which is made from pears. It has an individual flavour and the faintly golden colour of champagne.

The board met to consider the problem of the glut of perry. 'We shall never get rid of the stuff locally,' one of them remarked gloomily. 'It's cluttering up the cellars and at the present rate of sales it could be years before we get rid of it. Trouble is, most people know cider and plenty like it, but outside Somerset, whoever has heard of perry? What on earth are we to do about it?'

'Advertise it nationally,' piped up one of the younger sons. 'Get hold of a smart London advertising agent. Give the stuff a fancy name. Stick an attractive label on the bottle. If we can only think up the right slogan we can create a new market.'

This revolutionary idea caused his father, uncles and grandfather to ponder deeply. There could be something in it, they decided. They had never dabbled in the deep waters of national advertising but they were shrewd enough businessmen to realize that with the right slogan, the catchy symbol and a massive publicity campaign they might get away with it. Obviously it would cost money. How much they did not know. Men of lesser foresight, cogitating thus in a sleepy country town, might well have decided against such a gamble. After all, it could set them back many thousands of pounds with little result. On the other hand if the slogan and the symbol rang the bell, fortune was theirs. They decided to send an expedition to London.

So two younger members of the firm were sent to London to sound out the possibilities. They decided to go to a top advertising firm called Masius and Ferguson. They were a firm of American origin which within recent years has made its mark in London.

When the young Showerings arrived at the impressive building in Berkeley Square which houses these go-getting 'ad-men' they got into the lift, pressed the button and started off for the top floor where Masius and Ferguson roosted. Halfway up the lift stuck. So they opened the door and got out. Facing them was a door which bore in large letters the inviting words ADVERTISING AGENTS. They opened the door and walked in – to be warmly received by that other eminent firm of advertising agents, Messrs. J. Walter Thompson, Ltd. They realized their mistake and bowed themselves out.

They then plodded up flight after flight of steps to the top floor and found, finally, the eyrie of Masius and Ferguson. There they were received by Mr Wynne Williams, who was Number Two in the organization. They put their problems to him. He pondered them deeply. He questioned them on the history, structure and trade of their company. He got the picture. Then he said, 'Gentlemen, my board will consider your problem very carefully. We shall draw up a scheme which I hope will commend itself to you. Then I will come and see you. Meanwhile thank *you* for having the courtesy to come all this way to see us. Good day to you.'

Wynne Williams, who has a remarkably clear, astute and constructive mind considered the problem carefully with Mr Masius. Neither of them were very impressed by the prospects. Here was an old-fashioned but reputable country firm with no more than a local reputation loaded with a glut of stuff which they could not sell and which not one person in a hundred had ever heard of, let alone drunk. It did not seem to promise any great rewards.

However, nothing daunted, a week or so later Wynne Williams and one of his young assistants set off for Somerset in his motor-car. It was a long drive. They stopped two or three times on the way to refresh themselves, to consider the problem and to debate how much they could charge the clients for their services. To put over the scheme would obviously mean a good deal of expenditure of their own firm's time and money. What sort of fee would an old-fashioned country firm be prepared to pay? Could they ask £3,000 which would show little enough profit? Dare they raise the fee as high as £5,000, which would make the work worth while? Above all, what were to be the symbol and the slogan? With these questions buzzing in their brains they met the board of Showerings. They put it to them that whereas a champagne cider made from apples sold well under the name of pomagne, nobody has yet tried to market a champagne cider made from pears. It was not the slightest use trying to market it as perry. People might confuse it with Perrier, the mineral water.

However, they put up a scheme which the Showerings, somewhat to their surprise, accepted. Then they set off on the return journey to London, still searching their minds for a symbol and a slogan. They stopped on the way at several hostelries to refresh themselves. And, if my surmise is correct, it was in one pleasant old country inn that they saw a charming young girl, bubbling with the gaiety of youth, toss off a glass of champagne and say: 'Oh, this is good! I wish we could afford to drink it every day.' She had the sprightliness of a lamb in spring, the grace of a gazelle. There are lots of young girls like that.

So when they got back to London, the little dancing fawn, the dappled baby deer which today is the emblem of Babycham was born on the drawing board of a commercial artist and the name Babycham was invented.

They returned to Somerset soon after, complete with the symbol of the dancing fawn and armed with the irresistible selling name of Babycham. The Showering board agreed to the fee of £5,000 without demur.

Babycham, heralded by a fanfare of inspired publicity, burst upon the London market. It swept the market. Sales rocketed. One small final touch of genius clinched its selling popularity.

Wynne Williams had the bright idea of suggesting to Showering that in addition to marketing the new 'champagne' to publicans they should also sell, with each case of bottles, a consignment of specially-made wine glasses which had hollow stems. This meant that when a Sweet Young Thing raised her glass of bubbly to her lips extra bubbles coursed down the hollow stem. This not only enlivened the pear wine, but it gave the bewitched drinker an extra zip of enjoyment.

Thus a great advertising idea and a great national selling campaign which reaped a fortune for Showering was born from a couple of bright ideas.

The climax to this fairy-tale story came some time afterwards when Masius and Ferguson and Showering had each reaped their golden harvest. Wynne Williams was invited to pay another visit to Somerset to be entertained to luncheon by the Showering family. He set off in his old Armstrong Siddeley with his young colleague. They parked the motor-car outside the Showering office. When the luncheon was over the Chairman of Showerings said, 'Mr Wynne Williams, as a little token of appreciation of your brilliant advertising campaign which has brought this company enormous new markets and put us really on the map, I, on behalf of my colleagues on the board would like to make you a little present.'

'Good heavens, no,' Wynne William expostulated. 'You have paid us extremely well for our services. You've done well out of the new development and so have we. I'm perfectly happy, and so is my company. Its' a charming thought to offer me a present but I couldn't possibly accept it.'

'Afraid it's a bit too late for you to say no, Mr Wynne

Williams,' said the chairman. 'Look out of the window into the courtyard. There is your present.'

Wynne Williams rose from the table, walked over to the window and looked out. There, gleaming in the sun, sat a magnificent Rolls-Royce. He capitulated.

His young colleague drove the Armstrong Siddeley back to London. Wynne Williams, feeling a little bit like Caesar returning to Rome after the conquest of Britain, sat at the wheel of his new chariot and, eating up the miles between Somerset and London with smooth and effortless speed, purred superbly to a stop outside his offices in Berkeley Square. At that precise moment Mr Masius, his boss, debouched with stately tread from the front door of the offices and marched towards his own ancient Daimler which was waiting for him at the kerbside. He stopped, petrified, as Wynne Williams stepped out of his lordly Rolls.

'Whose car is that? he demanded.

'Mine,' said Wynne Williams briefly.

Masius changed colour. 'Where on earth did you get it – and how?' he demanded.

Oh, just a present from a grateful client,' said Wynne Williams airily.

Mr Masius grunted, stepped into his Daimler and drove off with a deeply thoughtful look on his face. I have reason to believe that this was why, although Mr Masius could well afford a Rolls, he stuck to his Daimlers thereafter.

The human crowning point of this remarkable success story was provided by my old friend Bob Foster, the head of Colgate-Palmolive, who never minced his words:

'Best thing that ever happened, this Babycham,' he said tersely. 'You know, Bill, what happens at these office parties. All the nice little girls turn up and all the low-life chaps lie in wait for 'em. They fill 'em up with port and lemon and the girls love it. It tastes sweet and nice but before they know where they are, they're tiddly. Next thing that happens is that they're pregnant – or sick. Then we have a lot of the girl staff away from work.

'Now this stuff Babycham has lots of bubbles. Its' sweet to

taste. It makes 'em feel bright and gay but the alcoholic content is so low that they never lose their heads. It's the young girl's best drink.

'Come on, old cock, let's have a bottle of Bollinger to toast it!'

Today the Showering family are millionaires. Their bubbly drink, which they do not pretend is any rival of champagne, has established its own unique niche in the drinking life of the nation. It does nobody any harm but it did do Wynne Williams a lot of good.

Before we leave the field of 'Ad-Men and Odd Men' I cannot resist telling the tale of my odd little mission to New York during that extraordinary period when the whole of the United States was in the grip of Prohibition. It was a crime to make a drink, sell a drink or take a drink. The result was a fantastic trade in the sale of illicit liquor known at that time as 'bootlegging.' Genuine liquor such as Scotch or Irish Whisky, champagne or authentic French or German wines fetched fabulous prices. 'Home-made' spirits of death-dealing power were sold under the counter in astronomical quantities. They included every sort of raw spirit. The result was that many who drank them either went blind, or raving mad or committed suicide. The death toll was quite appalling. Meanwhile the 'bootleg barons', the men behind the trade in illicit liquor, made huge fortunes. They had their undercover salesmen, their spies, their police contacts who were bribed heavily, and their private little armies of armed thugs. Murder was their common weapon.

The atmosphere when I arrived in New York was like nothing that this century has known before or since. I walked straight into Prohibition. Something quite new to my nature! I went straight to the apartment of Leslie Randall, the *Daily Express* chief correspondent in New York. Everything had been laid on in lavish style. There, to greet me, were those three great journalists, Quentin Reynolds, who later became perhaps the most famous American war correspondent in London where he shone as an outspoken friend and champion of this country, Miss Margaret Lane, notable not only as a journalist but as an author, and Miss Dixie Tighe, one of the most formidable women journalists in

America. Dixie was, as they say, a tough baby. There were also, as is the American way, a couple of statuesquely seductive blondes whose mission apparently was to entertain me in my private moments. Their smiles of welcome would have fetched a robin off its perch.

Miss Tighe stepped forward, shook me warmly by the hand, turned on our host and with a sweeping gesture said, 'You can throw those two blondes out! This man Needham is *my* baby! I'll look after him.' She gave the blondes one withering imperious glance, and said, 'You can get out of here.' They scuttled like rabbits.

The drink at that little welcoming party was genuine Scotch. I am afraid I took it for granted. Within the next few days I was to realize that I had been drinking pure gold.

'I hope you've got a case of this put aside for me in my room,' I said brightly to Leslie Randall.

'Sure,' said Leslie, 'There's a case of the stuff in your room. But not real Scotch. This is all we have of that. You've got a case of gin.'

'That'll do,' said I gratefully. 'Whose – Gordon's or Booth's? I hope it's the right stuff.'

'Sure,' said Leslie again, 'I made it myself – in the bath!' That was enough. I had heard enough lurid tales of blindness, lunacy and suicide to warn me off anybody's home-made hooch. Randall's vitiated bath-water went down the plug-hole.

Among the victims of home-made hooch at about that time were two close friends of Lord Beaverbrook. They died agonizing deaths. This made such a lasting impression on 'the little man' that, for some years after Prohibition had ended, he insisted that every bottle of whisky from which he drank should first be put in front of him with the seal unbroken and the cork still in. Once when a wine waiter put a bottle of whisky on the table in front of him with the cork out Beaverbrook said abruptly, 'Take it away. I'll not drink it. All corks must be drawn in front of me.' This was in spite of the fact that the whisky was his own favourite brand, a well-known Scotch whisky known as 'Best Procurable.'

In passing, I must pay a tribute to that indomitable woman,

Dixie Tighe. Not only did she dance me off my feet, show me every side of New York life and introduce me to a host of nice people, but, when the Second World War came, she showed herself to be a woman of heroic courage. She went out to the Far East as a special war correspondent where she wore full military uniform and was under fire many times with the American Forces. I am told that she never showed the slightest sign of fear.

She came to London at the height of the Blitzkreig when the city was bombed and set on fire night after night. Most people spent the night in cellars, air-raid shelters, tube stations or heavily reinforced rooms. Not so Dixie. She took the top flat in one of the tallest buildings in Dover Street, from which vantage point she could see the fires of London whilst the whole building rocked with the concussion of heavy bombs. She went out in the streets in a tin hat whilst shrapnel, bomb fragments, bricks and broken glass were raining down. I thought I had a pretty good baptism of heavy gun-fire during two years of trench warfare in Flanders, but I am bound to confess that I felt dead scared more than once when taking an evening stroll with Dixie. That woman did not know the meaning of fear. Alas, like too many people in journalism who lead lives of high tension and work at top speed for all hours, she died of a stroke half-way through life.

One odd little side-light lightened that hectic visit in the bootleg days. Leslie Randall went out of his way to get me a special ticket for one of the big baseball games, at the Yankee Stadium. This was a great honour. Tickets were at a premium.

'One word of warning,' Leslie said sternly. 'You wear an eye-glass at home in London. The seat we've got you should be in a good place, but I can't guarantee it. So wherever you may sit I do warn you first of all not to wear your eyeglass and secondly not to say in your very English voice "What a jolly good game of rounders!" You'll be lynched.'

So, reluctantly, for the next few days I kept my eyeglass – which is a necessity – safely stowed away in a waistcoat pocket on the end of its cord.

Finally I got tired of having to fumble for my spectacles, fish them out of my pocket and stick them on my nose every time I had to read a newspaper or study a menu.

So, exasperated, in a crowded restaurant where we were getting little service, I whipped out my eyeglass, stuck it defiantly in my eye and glared sternly at the head waiter. The effect was electric. Waiters scuttled at us like rabbits. We got superb service. So the eyeglass remained firmly in place for the rest of my visit. It worked like a charm.

My American hosts and guests were not only dumbfounded by the speed and efficiency of the service evoked by that little circle of glass, but they were paralysed when they heard me referred to by deferential head-waiters as 'the English lord'.

Ad-men, contrary to the general opinion held among journalists, are human. Here is a little story which illustrates this often disregarded truth. The London Press Exchange is one of the better-known and long-established advertising agencies. It was established well over half a century ago by one Reggie Sykes whose family are still active in its direction.

Just before the Second World War one of its minor executives, called in those days a space-buyer, was one Freddie Gooding. Tall, balding, with a dome of a head, somewhat pot-bellied and with a bulbous nose, he looked precisely like that Dickensian character, Mr Micawber. Moreover, he was a great authority on Dickens. He could quote chapter and verse concerning any character in Dickens's works. Literally, he lived in that period. He was also highly knowledgeable on pictures and china. Altogether a man of cultivated taste.

His other taste was for most forms of drink, especially port wine. He knew the vintages as well as he knew his Dickens characters. His lunch, whether he was eating alone, entertaining a client or the centre of a bunch of admiring colleagues, was invariably topped up by two large glasses of vintage port. Add to this the fact that he was an engaging conversationalist, and it was not surprising that whenever Freddie Gooding entered a pub or a restaurant he was the centre of a little circle of ad-men, journalists and business-men.

Unfortunately when Freddie was in his cups he not infrequently offended the landlord of his current hostelry or took offence himself. He would thereupon flounce out, followed by his little coterie and descend upon another pub. The word swiftly went round that the White Lion was out of favour but the Red Lion was in.

Freddie attracted so many followers that his departure from any pub meant that the landlord suffered a sizeable hole in his takings. This happy state of convivial affairs had gone on for years. Despite his nose and and his intake of port Freddie not only got business but he was an astonishing encyclopaedia of newspaper and advertising facts and figures. There was no Audit Bureau of Circulation in those days. Advertisers had almost to guess the circulation of a newspaper. Freddie knew all the answers. He could tell you accurately the approximate sales of any newspaper from John o'Groats to Land's End.

Then came, like a small menacing cloud on the horizon, the bustling energetic figure of Major Harrison. Major Harrison was an accountant. He had all the accountant's cold-blooded reverence for facts, figures, statistics, time-sheets, in-put, out-put and the rest. He was, one would have said, a de-humanized calculating machine. He was the computer in human form. He cast a jaundiced eye upon the convivial activities of Freddie Gooding. Freddie, in the eyes of Major Harrison, broke all the rules of efficient business.

Since Major Harrison was Managing Director, this clearly spelt disaster for Freddie. The chopper would fall on him at any moment. Freddie was warned by more than one colleague that he was not in favour. The sack was just round the corner. Blandly he ignored all the warnings. Each day at half past twelve he issued forth from his office followed by his little cavalcade of admirers and descended, talking, gesticulating, joking, upon his favourite pub of the moment. There the personal parliament of Freddie Gooding remained in session for a couple of hours or so.

No matter where his new-found pub might be its name and location went round Fleet Street like a bush-fire. The smoke signals went up – and the tribesmen gathered at the festal pot. Major Harrison fumed. His warnings were disregarded. To him this was unforgivable. He sharpened his chopper.

Then came the war. Business, including advertising and news-papers, was in a ferment. Anything might happen at any time. It was no time, therefore to get rid of an experienced, elderly mem-

ber of the staff when all the young men on the staff were liable
to be called up to military service at short notice. Freddie Gooding won an unexpected respite.

There followed the air raids on London. Offices had their
own fire-watchers on the roofs of their buildings and in air-raid
shelters or basements. Freddie Gooding was the first to volunteer.
Major Harrison, a First World War soldier with Regular Army
training was not far behind him. Soon they found themselves
sharing the same night-long duties when bombs fell, buildings
disintegrated, whole streets were swept by flames, and dead and
wounded civilians were nightly casualties in hundreds.

Freddie Gooding stood up to it all with cheerfulness, bravery
and unlimited philosophy. He discoursed fluently on Dickens as
the anti-aircraft guns roared and the buildings shuddered to the
roar of exploding bombs. He talked with knowledge and taste of
old pictures and fine china. The row going on outside disturbed
him not a bit. Major Harrison found himself, almost against
his will, a fascinated listener. He began to realize why Freddie,
in the happy lunch-hours of peacetime, had attracted his personal
'congregation' of such diverse people. He was filled with admiration for Gooding's courage, his knowledge and, above
all, his gentleness of manner. This blossomed into a genuine
affectionate friendship.

When the war came to an end, young men, eager for jobs,
poured out of the Services into business. Freddie was getting old.
He was the first to realize that he would have to make way for
young blood. He faced the prospect with his usual calm philosophy and waited for the worst. It did not happen. The major,
who had so often threatened to sack him, was in no hurry to do
so. Their friendship, cemented among the hideous uproar of
bombs, fires and gun-fire, endured.

Finally, some years later, Freddie was gracefully retired to
spend the rest of his old age in vinous philosophy, on a far
larger pension than he had ever expected.

The last I heard of Freddie he was happily growing chrysan-
themums in the country, where, as you might expect, he had
established himself as a top authority on that particular flower.

One day the major arrived at the garden gate in the Rolls-

Royce which is the badge of top ad-men. There was Freddie, tying up his blooms on his hands and knees. Major Harrison walked up the garden path, patted his old friend on the back, and invited himself indoors for a cup of tea. He enquired about Freddie's gardening prowess.

'Well, I've just got a couple of firsts and a third prize,' said Freddie modestly. The major gazed approvingly at the row of silvercups which decorated the sideboard.

'But I don't like to see you down on your hands and knees, Freddie,' he remarked. 'It's not like you.'

'It doesn't do my old knees any good, either,' Freddie remarked, 'but I've got to do it.'

'What's the alternative?' Major Harrison asked.

'Oh, a greenhouse,' said Freddie. 'But that's a bit beyond my means.'

The major enquired gently what size of greenhouse he needed and what the cost was likely to be. Freddie, unsuspecting, gave him the figures. The major shook hands and left.

Four days later a splendid greenhouse arrived, was erected in the garden and Freddie was transported to his little Seventh Heaven. Who says that ad-men are not human?

Part of one's job as a top executive on the advertising side of a great newspaper is that one is frequently called upon to make speeches at public banquets and other functions. These speeches can cover a wide range of subjects. The great thing is not only to know your facts but to have a repertoire of allegedly funny stories and anecdotes which will raise a laugh. Once the audience starts laughing, you're safe. I therefore had my little stock of quips and stories.

When I was in America I collected a number of transatlantic stories, one of which had the supreme virtue of being true. It concerned the visit to America of Sir Samuel Hoare (later Lord Templewood), the famous statesman. This anecdote I duly stored in my memory for future use. Little did I realize when later I trotted it out at a highly distinguished banquet in the City of London that my reward would be the reddest face in England.

It came about thus. Mr Hayman, Chairman of the Distillers' Company became the newly elected Master of the Vintners'

Company. A grand banquet was to be held in the Vintners'
Hall in the City, to celebrate the fact. Mr Hayman was good
enough to invite me as his personal guest of honour. I sat on
his left side at the high table. On his right hand sat the Lord
Mayor of London. The rest of the top table included that wonderful orator and charming man Mr Bruce, Premier of Australia
and one of the greatest of Empire statesmen, plus a most impressive herbaceous border of politicians, soldiers, sailors, millionaires,
business chiefs, legal luminaries and the rest.

I had to 'say a few words'.

When my turn came I made the appropriate noises and then
groped in my mind for a story to raise a laugh.

'Gentlemen,' I said, 'I am reminded by this illustrious gather-
ing of a story which I recently heard in America concerning the
visit of that eminent Minister of State, Sir Samuel Hoare, to
America some years ago. A committee of Senators was formed to
receive him. The chairman drilled them beforehand: "Gennelmen," he said, "I understand on good authority from England
that Sir Samuel Hoare, the great English statesman, is a little
tender about the implications of his surname. That is understand-
able. Therefore, gennelmen, when you are introduced to him, I
suggest that you do not use his surname. Each of you should
extend the hand of friendship and greet him cordially as Sir
Samuel. That, I understand, is good English etiquette. Just
forget the surname and all that it might mean to a dirty mind.'
The Senators, thus instructed, acted accordingly.

'Came the great day. Sir Samuel Hoare was greeted by an impressive reception committee of Senators from all over the States.
One after the other they bowed, shook hands and extended their
cordial greetings to Sir Samuel.

'All except the Senator from Dallas, Texas. He was at the
end of the line. He determined to trump the rest of the pack. Ex-
tending his hand, he said with a beaming smile: "Happy to
meet you, Sir Samuel. When you come to Dallas, Texas, you
will be assured of the most cordial welcome, Sir Samuel – and
that goes for Lady W. Also." '

The roar of applause, the tidal wave of hysterical laughter
which greeted this story flummoxed me. The story was funny

enough in its way, but surely it could not deserve such uproarious hilarity. I sat down, perplexed. My neighbour whispered in my ear, 'That rang the bell. The Lord Mayor's nearly killing himself.'

'Why' I asked innocently.

'Why? Surely you know? His name's Hoare.'

Looking back over more than fifty years of my life in Fleet Street, I can say truthfully that I would not have had it otherwise. I have enjoyed every minute. It is a far cry from the small boy who burst into tears at that house in Cricklewood when a hansom-cab called in the dark mystery of a winter night to whisk my father off to the unknown perils of that unknown abyss called Fleet Street, to the present day when I am, I suppose, something of an Elder Statesman in the Street of Adventure. I am proud to end my career as Personal Consultant on Advertising, the life-blood of a newspaper, to 'the young', Sir Max Aitken, the son of that lovable, unforgettable, invincible and utterly human man, Lord Beaverbrook.

There will never be another Beaverbrook. He was unique. But his spirit and his crusading genius is lit, as a new flame, in the heart and brain of his son. Whilst such men endure, the future of the Press, which is the ordinary man's great safety valve of freedom of expression, will survive. It will be a bad day, a disastrous day, for this country if the freedom of the Press is ever constricted or muzzled.

For my own part I can say with all sincerity that the Street of Adventure, which beckoned me in those far-off boyish days, has turned out to be a Street of Adventure in the true sense. I do not regret one moment.

Index